Other Avon Books by
N. E. Genge
THE UNOFFICIAL X-FILES COMPANION II

THE X-FILES LEXICON

N. E. GENGE

AVON BOOKS NEW YORK

THE X-FILES LEXICON is an original publication of Avon Books. This work has never before appeared in book form.

Photographs on pages 4, 6, 8, 10, 11, 12, 16, 17, 19, 20, 22, 23, 25, 29, 32, 38, 40, 42, 43, 44, 46, 51, 57, 59, 65, 66, 71, 72, 78, 80, 82, 83, 84, 87, 88, 90, 96, 101, 103, 104, 106, 107, 108, 109, 111, 112, 115, 117, 118, 121, 122, 123, 124, 126, 128, 129 by Jeffrey L. Krasner, © 1996. Photographs on pages 1, 36, 49, 73, 75, 102, 130 © Fox Broadcasting Company/courtesy Photofest. Photographs on pages 33, 37, 54, 60, 67, 95, 98, 100 © Fox Broadcasting Company/courtesy Everett Collection. Photograph on page 53 © Globe Photos, Inc. and Fitzroy Barrett.

Jeffrey L. Krasner would like to thank the following: Stock's Eye Studios, Ashley K. Lamb, Carol McDonald, Rose and Paul Krasner, Blair A. Thoma, Michele Zaluski, T. and F. Yastrzemski, Hallmark Institute of Photography.

AVON BOOKS
A division of
The Hearst Corporation
1350 Avenue of the Americas
New York, New York 10019

Copyright © 1997 by N.E. Genge
Published by arrangement with the author
Text design by Stanley S. Drate/Folio Graphics Co., Inc.
Visit our website at http://AvonBooks.com
ISBN: 0-380-79023-8

Library of Congress Cataloging in Publication Data:
Genge, Ngaire.
    The X-files lexicon / N.E. Genge.
        p.   cm.
    1. X-files (Television program)   I. Title.
PN1992.77.X22G48   1997   96-46336
791.45'72—dc21   CIP

First Avon Books Trade Printing: March 1997

AVON TRADEMARK REG. U.S. PAT. OFF. AND IN OTHER COUNTRIES, MARCA REGISTRADA, HECHO EN U.S.A.

Printed in the U.S.A.

QPM   10 9 8 7 6 5 4 3 2 1

For Michael,
who helps me find the humor in everything—
even *The X-Files*

ACKNOWLEDGMENTS

So many people . . . so little space.

Jeff Krasner, for being a great short-order photographer and one hell of
a nice guy.
Robert Stock, for space, scanners, studios; Spud, who made me laugh,
and his wonderful wife, who let him come out and play.
Stephen S. Power and the gang at Avon Books for timely comments and
keen eyes.
Ling Lucas and Ed Vesneske, Jr., who thought this little book might be
fun.
Paula "Cuzzie" Moulton and her family, for years of laughter and sharing, and for their continued support.
And Peter, who makes the end of my workdays so very worthwhile.

X CONTENTS X

NUMBERS

$1.75

The spurious refund from a broken pay phone Skinner's would-be assassin harassed a waitress for. (Piper Maru)

109

The usual body temperature of Cecil L'Ively, the *X-Files* version of the Human Torch. (Fire)

13

The number of minutes that Jack Willis was officially dead. (Lazarus)

147

Number of stars decorating one of Scully's less "power-suited" blouses. (Roland)

15626

A useful number if you're trying to break into the files of a dead rocket scientist. (Roland)

2

1—Number of daughters Margaret Scully has sat next to in the Critical Care Unit and eventually bought headstones for. **2**—Number of blood types found on Lucy Householder's uniform. (Oubliette) **3**—Number of people who've driven their cars into trees after seeing something unpalatable in their rearview mirrors. (The List, Fresh Bones) **4**—Number of times we've seen Mulder find packages in a car he thought he'd locked. (Young at Heart, Fire) **5**—Number of heartbeats Mulder insisted were visible on the EKG of Jack

Willis. (Lazarus) **6**—Number of consenting adults Mulder spied on before getting his jaw rearranged by one of them. (3) **7**—Number of people Mulder claims survived at a remote volcanology site on Mount Avalon. (Firewalker)

20

Denomination of the bill you don't want to hand Byers of the Lone Gunmen, not if you want it back in one piece! (E.B.E.)

27

Number of people who managed to come down with a one-in-a-million disease in the tiny town of Dudley, Arkansas, home of Chaco Chicken. (Our Town)

28

The tender age Mulder had achieved by the time he left the FBI Academy at Quantico.

$29.95

The cost of a guaranteed, genuine alien autopsy video, shipping and handling, state and federal taxes not included. (Nisei)

200

Number of missile silos Mulder and Scully would have had to check out if the Cigarette-Smoking Man hadn't decided to take over from them himself. (Apocrypha)

220

The sort of IQ that creates sociopathic machines—then defends their right to life. (Ghost in the Machine)

265

The sort of IQ that shouldn't be handed out to women who spend their spare moments biting into their guards' eyeballs. (Eve)

2,000

Number of volts zapped through Neetch the day he died. (The List)

$39.92

What Incredible Inventions will charge you for Spray-on Hair. (Beyond the Sea)

$300

How much credit Madam Zirinka was willing to advance Mulder on his Visa Gold card. Guess he was closer to his limit than most of us like to be. (Syzygy)

$4

What it costs for the first hour of parking under the Watergate Hotel and Convention Center. (Little Green Men)

$49.95

The price of Mulder's latest crime-fighting gadget, a laser pointer. (Soft Light)

5

Number of men Neetch promised would die. (The List)

6

1—In the real world, there are a mere four DNA nucleotides possible. In the X-Files universe, there are at least six. (The Erlenmeyer Flask) **2**—Number of years Special Agent Dana Scully had been away from the Roman Catholic Church before a little boy named Kevin Kreider, and the "abnormal" body of "St. Owen," sent her in search of spiritual guidance instead of scientific answers. (Revelations)

60

Roland Fuller's apparent IQ. (Roland)

302

Internal FBI forms authorizing travel expenses. Think Mulder filed one for the ATV he commandeered in Alaska? (Conduit, Colony)

340

The number of years John Barnett was supposed to serve in jail. (Young at Heart)

56

The number of chromosomes required to produce a modern-day Eve. The rest of us manage with 46. (Eve)

65

Number of the parallel where vessels like the *Flying Dutchmen* or U.S. Navy vessels named *Ardent* hang out. (Død Kalm)

7

The size shoeprint Skinner sported after he was beaten soundly by a tiny office clerk named Holly. (Pusher)

75

The case resolution percentage that allows loose-cannon agents to pursue their own cases without serious intervention by the powers-that-be. (Tooms)

731

Name of a unit of Japanese doctors who evidently had some difficulty translating the Hippocratic Oath. (Nisei)

8

Number of layers of kevlar that John Barnett's bullet pierced on its flight toward Scully's chest. (Young at Heart)

$8.50

Cost of lunch for three FBI agents. (Ghost in the Machine)

935

Locker number where John Barnett stashed the "fountain of youth." (Young at Heart)

$1,000,000

What kidnapper Lula Phillips thought Scully was worth to the FBI. (Lazarus)

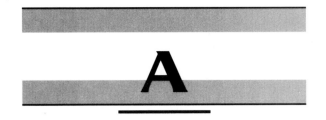

A

"a belching fool"

How Darren Peter Oswald's mother described her only child. (D.P.O.)

ABS brakes

Spoiled Darren Oswald's fun out on County Road A-7. (D.P.O.)

"adult" magazines

The reading material most likely to be found under Mulder's mattress or lurking in the bottom drawer of his desk. (The Jersey Devil)

Adult Video News

According to Scully, one of Mulder's favorite magazines. (Beyond the Sea)

agape

The condition in which Scully's jaw is often found.

"Agent Orange of the Nineties"

Gulf War Syndrome (E.B.E.)

airbag

While the whole "face in the airbag" plotline of one episode left some viewers scratching their heads, there's no doubt Scully's airbag came in pretty handy when Donny Pfaster ran her off the road. (Avatar, Irresistible)

ajar

The condition in which Mulder's front door is often found.

alley

The accommodation for which Mulder gave up a room—with HBO—at Atlantic City's Galaxy Gateway Hotel. (The Jersey Devil)

alone

The stupid, if traditional, way to investigate crime scenes, to track suspected serial killers, and to attempt arrests in the X-Files universe. (2SHY)

amaru urns

Best left where they're found. (Teso dos Bichos)

Ambassador Hotel

Bad place to pick up women. (Avatar)

AmWay salesman

Career Mulder declares himself unfit for after a door-to-door search for serial killer Virgil Incanto. (2SHY)

animal control officer

Of all occupations, the only one likely to provide Eugene Tooms with appetizers as well as a paycheck. (Squeeze)

ankle-grabbing

Mulder's least favorite part of being a special agent. (The Host)

ankle holster

Mulder's response to the all-too-frequent sound of his usual sidearm hitting the floor. (Revelations)

answering machine

Possessed, answered, and "cracked," this telephone add-on has been as much trouble as convenience for residents of the X-Files universe. In one episode the message on Mulder's machine even changed overnight—despite the fact that Mulder wasn't home! (The Walk, The Blessing Way, Young at Heart, Colony)

anthropomancy

Divination by examination of human entrails. (Clyde Bruckman's Final Repose)

anti-freeze

The one substance Scully can identify without recourse to the FBI labs—although it will, of course, get there eventually (D.P.O.)

anti-Waltons

Mulder's description of Scully's whiz-bang theory on the inheritable nature of psychotic personality traits and, contrary to Scully's own scientific beliefs, fingerprints. (Squeeze)

armpits

Bad places to find little black nodules. (Ice)

astronaut

What Mulder wanted to be when he grew up. (Space)

Atlantic City

Happy hunting grounds for the Jersey Devil. (The Jersey Devil)

Arlington National Cemetery

Where Deep Throat was buried, and Sergeant Leonard Trimble wasn't. (Little Green Men, The Walk)

Aurora Project

The high-security aircraft and surveillance project that the Department of Defense has actually, under heavy pressure and stacks of evidence, granted *may* exist. (Deep Throat)

autoerotic asphyxiation

Clyde Bruckman's tongue-in-cheek inference of Mulder's eventual cause of death. (Clyde Bruckman's Final Repose)

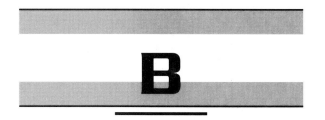

B-rate monster films

After "adult" videos, Mulder's preferred late-night TV fare. (Tooms)

Bach

The musician Mulder "lives for"—at least when the room he's in is being bugged. (Little Green Men)

backwards

How to listen to telephone messages left by Rappo. (The Walk)

Dr. Bambi

An entomologist with a taste for short shorts and unique explanations for UFO sightings—both of which intrigued Mulder. (War of the Coprophages)

Dr. Chester Ray Banton

The man who gave whole new meanings to the term "personal space," and the first person to frighten the daylights out of the imperturbable X. (Soft Light)

barbecue

You might want to consider your reply to such an invitation rather carefully if the offer comes from someone in Dudley, Arkansas, or involves a Chaco Chicken. (Our Town)

Barney

Second only to the CIA as the most "heinous" force of our time. (E.B.E.)

basement

1—Dark, dank hole where you don't want to hear the click of camera gear going off. (Oubliette) 2—At FBI headquarters, home of the agency's Most Unwanted investigative team. (The X-Files: Pilot) 3—Site of a highly unusual mushroom farm. (Excelsius Dei) 4—One-stop dining facility for snakes of unusual size and appetites. (Die Hand Die Verletzt)

Basement, THE

Repository of everything from nasal implants to recovered alien tissue, the Pentagon Basement is Mulder's wet dream. (The X-Files: Pilot, The Erlenmeyer Flask)

bath

All the bubbles in the world wouldn't make this an enjoyable experience for any woman if Donny Pfaster were manning the taps. (Irresistible)

bathroom

1—Natural habitat for any fat-sucking, liver-eating, or shape-shifting mutants with an unnatural taste for agents named Scully. (2SHY, Squeeze, Shapes) 2—Site of an unnaturally high number of unnatural deaths. (731, War of the Coprophages, Avatar, etc.)

"beacon in the night"

Mulder's description of his superior, Assistant Director Walter S. Skinner. (Nisei)

bed of nails

In Dr. Blockhead's residence, "more comfortable than a futon." (Humbug)

bedwetters

Criminals considerably easier to find than the ones that killed Melissa Scully. (Piper Maru)

bellhop

The last person to let in your hotel room at Le Damfino Hotel. (Clyde Bruckman's Final Repose)

bellies

Frequently mistaken by aliens and foreign scientists for balloons. (Nisei, Ascension)

bets

Not a good thing to make in San Francisco's Chinatown. (Hell Money)

"between two truths"

The most effective place to hide a lie. (E.B.E.)

"Beyond the Sea"

The haunting strains of Bobby Darin's classic took on a completely different tone when hummed by one of the few people to make Scully question her version of the Truth, Luther Boggs. (Beyond the Sea)

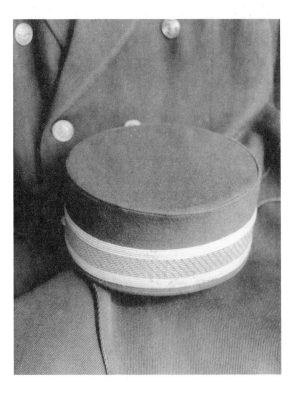

Big & Beautiful Chat Room
Bad place to pick up a guy. (2SHY)

Big Blue
Lake creature worth hunting if the writers stick your character with an annoying Pomeranian. (Quagmire)

bile
Substance that's impossible to remove from the tips of one's fingers without betraying one's cool exterior. (Squeeze)

bilge-cleaning
Aside from the muckiest job aboardships, a damn fine way to encounter enormous flukemen. (The Host)

bipolar condition
The ailment both Carl Wade and Daniel Trepkos supposedly suffered from, though neither showed any of that condition's symptoms. (Oubliette, Firewalker)

black hole season
Mulder's alternative to the "invisible elephant" theory. Scully wasn't buying either of them. (Fearful Symmetry)

"black-lunged-son-of-a-bitch"
Mulder's term of endearment for the Cigarette-Smoking Man (Anasazi)

blood drives
These and postal workers just don't mix in Franklin City, Pennsylvania. (Blood)

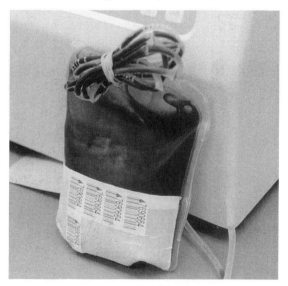

"blood-sucking worm, giant"
What wriggles its way through sewers throughout the state of New Jersey. (The Host)

"Bloody Mary"
The *last* thing you want to hear being sung in your bathroom. (Syzygy)

blue light bulbs
In conjunction with a windowpane and some masking tape, a method of contacting one's covert cronies. (E.B.E.)

Agent Mo Bocks
The only agent at the Bureau who could possibly be more "open-minded" than Fox Mulder. (Irresistible)

the "book"
Mulder threw out the copy he'd been given by the FBI after a fellow agent and a hostage died while Mulder was still following it. (Young at Heart)

"bonafide paranoiac"
Mulder's description of himself. (Revelations)

boxcars
The agent-sized version of a Roach Motel. (The Blessing Way, Anasazi, Nisei, 731)

Boys' Club
How Scully, with some justification, describes the FBI and law enforcement in general. (Soft Light, 2SHY)

"brain-sucking amoeba"
The Mount St. Helen's version of the green, glowing bugs the Dynamic Duo face during their "nice trip to the woods." (Darkness Falls)

"branched" DNA
The genetic anomaly that led Mulder to his first, albeit long-distance, meeting with the Thinker, and that nearly led Scully to her death. (One Breath)

bridges

A hazardous location to exchange dead alien tissue for live agents, or to trade sisters for partners. (The Erlenmeyer Flask, Colony)

bright lights

Whether from motorcycles, 4x4s, black helicopters, or UFOs, never a good portent when appearing suddenly in the night sky.

"bright, white place"

Accidental tourist location for the gals of MUFON and other abductees. (Nisei)

Brother Andrew

If not for Mulder's timely interruption, Scully might have found herself doing the "wild thing" with this less-than-brotherly member of the Kindred. (GenderBender)

Bug-of-the-Week

From maggots to cockroaches to alien worms that hide under Arctic ice stations,

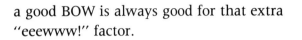
a good BOW is always good for that extra "eeewww!" factor.

bundt cake
What Mulder offers to send local law enforcement officers in order to obtain their assistance. (Conduit)

burnt paint
What you don't want to find on the top of your trailer after a trip to Lake Okobogee. (Conduit)

burnt treetops
Probably a good sign that you've picked the wrong campsite. (Conduit)

"butt munch"
Samantha's "term of endearment" for her older brother, Fox. (Little Green Men)

buzzard
The large, cowardly bird responsible for saving Mulder's life in a spray-painted gravel pit outside Vancouver. (The Blessing Way)

Byers
The Lone Gunman best known for his dull ties, staccato verbal delivery, and interest in video cameras that can be mounted atop common houseflies. (Blood)

campaigns of misinformation
What Mulder indulges in when he isn't "lying" to his superiors. (Shadows)

campsite #53
Lake Okobogee locale visited by the Morris family, two FBI agents, and aliens. (Conduit)

cannibalism
Chosen diet of several X-Filean villains.

canine cuspids
Joe Goodensnake gave new meaning to the "canine" part of the phrase. (Shapes)

capital punishment
Featured twice on *The X-Files*. Once it was the beginning of a case, in the other it was a fitting end. (The List, Beyond the Sea)

car rental agreements
Considering the number of cars Mulder rents, something you'd think he'd take better care of. (Apocrypha)

Celebrity Skin

The magazine that nudged the August issue of *The Lone Gunman* off Mulder's toilet tank. (Blood)

cellular phone

Winner of the Most Frequently Lost Equipment Award, the same competition in which guns came a tight second and computers took third. This handy piece of equipment was deemed "untraceable" when Scully was kidnapped, but the same phone became a convenient link when the Cigarette-Smoking Man decided to track down Scully. (Lazarus, Anasazi)

cerulean blue

If he'd known Pusher would be such an apt backseat driver, Detective Frank Burst would likely have paid more attention to his driver's wardrobe choices and suggested a less "calming" shade. (Pusher)

Chadwick's

Where Skinner ordered the blue plate special but got a stomach full of lead instead. (Piper Maru)

Ambrose Chapel

Other than a nod to Hitchcock, who had a character of the same name, a quick-change artist extraordinaire who owes Scully a new set of shoes. (Colony)

cherub

What Mulder asks Scully for after she's finished the plaster cast of Oswald's shoe—preferably one that pees. (D.P.O.)

chicken coop

What Fox couldn't guard. (Young at Heart)

chicken corpses

One of the more disturbing decor elements to find in your mother-in-law's rooms. (The Calusari)

chicken feet

What you don't want to find "attached" to your service record. (Fresh Bones)

cigarettes

The ongoing symbol of all things nasty in X-Files land.

Cigarette-Smoking Man

A member of the Consortium, player in the shadow government, and controller of secrets, the Cigarette-Smoking Man balances precariously between his many loyalties.

That his life has been tied up rather intimately with the Mulder family is beyond doubt, though his role remains hidden from Fox.

While the extent of his reach is unknown, and his level of power shifts with each change of the political wind, he exerts considerable influence on an assistant director of the FBI and casually orders the death of almost anyone who stands in his way or who, like former subordinate Alex Krycek, becomes an embarrassing inconvenience.

Perhaps to secure his own position, or perhaps as his primary function, CSM expends considerable energy in locating and controlling the information that Mulder and Scully would call evidence.

classifieds

Good place to begin looking for masterless samurai with unusual skills. (Pusher)

the cleaners

Where you don't want to send your bagged and tagged evidence—not if you're looking for an office out of the basement. (Ghost in the Machine)

"click-click-click"

To Scully, the symptom of a bad phone line, but to Mulder, clandestine signals from his own personal Deep Throat. (Eve)

clocks

In the X-Files universe, these simple instruments show a disturbing trend to display 11:21 or 10:13.

clones

In terms of plot, a clear indicator that our agents are about to get in over their heads. If it's not the unearthly Samantha clones come to pluck the heartstrings of Fox Mulder, it's the Eves doing their best to convince both agents that they'd just as soon skip parenthood. (Colony, End Game, Eve)

"close"

Where Deep Throat liked to keep his friends. (Fallen Angel)

"closer"

Where Deep Throat advocated keeping one's enemies. (Fallen Angel)

cockroaches

The last thing you want to find in your house if you live in Miller's Grove. (War of the Coprophages)

Sir Arthur Conan Doyle's tombstone

Site of a "youthful indiscretion" between Mulder and Phoebe Green on a misty night. (Fire)

Connerville's local diner

Hangout for cops, mechanics, and scientists from the Astodorian Lightning Observatory. (D.P.O.)

conscience

According to Commodore Johansen, "the voices of the dead, trying to save us from our own damnation." (Piper Maru)

Consortium

A Boys' Club even older than the FBI that includes the Well-Manicured Man, the Cigarette-Smoking Man, and even young Alex Krycek in those admitted to its refined quarters in midtown Manhattan. Other than a rather intense shared interest in places like Roswell, abandoned missile silos in South Dakota, sunken ships in the mid-Pacific, and whatever might be lurking in Fox Mulder's head, these guys like to play their cards close to the vest—shuffling for power even among themselves.

Kim Cook

Skinner's personal assistant, she had enough on the ball to call in Scully when Skinner was shot. (Avatar, Piper Maru)

"cosmic G-spot"

Where Mulder and Scully find themselves when they take in small-town Comity on the weekend. (Syzygy)

constipation

The effect that talking with Mulder has on some people. (War of the Coprophages)

"crazy people howling at the moon"

Mulder's surprising description of people who believe in UFOs. (Conduit)

"the creeps"

What Lyle Parker got just after his father's cattle were attacked by creatures unknown—and just before he himself started growing long teeth and more fur than could be explained by a little testosterone imbalance. (Shapes)

cremation

If, as in the case of Scully's father, a ceremony undertaken posthumously and by choice, a fitting end to earthly life. If, on the other hand, it occurs *pre*-humously with the subject kicking and screaming all the way, it's the beginning of an X-File. (Beyond the Sea, Hell Money)

Roger Crockett

Appetizer for the Jersey Devil. (The Jersey Devil)

crop circles

Though Mulder flatly denounces the unusual grain patterns as frauds, in one episode he rethinks that claim after the entire Kindred community mysteriously disappears. (Fallen Angel, GenderBender)

"crunch-squeak"

Sound made by stepping on the scattered remains of a frozen ear. (Roland)

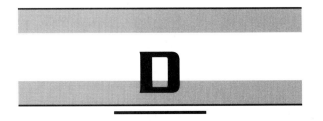

"Dana!"

Used only under extreme circumstances, like the death of her father or her kidnapping by demented maniacs, Scully's first name has escaped Mulder's lips only slightly less rarely than his has crossed hers. (Beyond the Sea, Lazarus, Ascension)

dark matter

Either a problem for theoretical physicists worldwide, or for carpet cleaners in the state of Virginia, or both. (Soft Light)

dates

Scully kept her one and only, but found it a drag. Mulder missed his and found nasty messages on his answering machine when he got home. (The Jersey Devil)

day-old jelly doughnuts

Darren Peter Oswald's idea of a come-on. (D.P.O.)

DEAD ALIEN! Truth or Humbug?

The video that made Special Agent Dana Scully a reluctant film star in a well-niched market. (Jose Chung's "From Outer Space")

Deadman's Hand

Three aces and a pair of eights, the hand Bruckman was dealt the night before his death. (Clyde Bruckman's Final Repose)

deals

What the Cigarette-Smoking Man "doesn't work." (Paper Clip)

death by garage-door opener

Proof that good writers can make even the most prosaic item dramatic. Of course, the same episode also added "savaged to death by roosters" to the numerous intriguing causes of death featured in *The X-Files*. (The Calusari)

debunk

What Chief Scott Blevins never *directly* asked Scully to do when she was assigned to Special Agent Fox Mulder and the X-Files he was investigating.

Deep Throat

From the time he first appeared carrying information about strange happenings at Ellens Air Force Base until Mulder watched him be laid to rest in Arlington, Deep Throat remained a mystery. His reasons for "assisting" Mulder remained his own, yet, despite being found out in more than one lie, he remained a trusted source and, unlike X, he never tried to beat Mulder senseless in an underground garage.

He claimed to have been a member of the CIA during the Vietnam conflict, was involved with William Mulder when they were younger men, and continued to hold a privileged position within the intelligence community until his death. He died with Scully watching on a bridge outside Washington while securing the release of a captured Mulder.

defacing library books

Crime Mulder suggests as the one most likely undertaken by the Lone Gunmen. (Anasazi)

defibrillator

One of the many careers open to a man with Darren Oswald's particular talents. (D.P.O.)

Die Bug Die!

Hot seller in Miller's Grove, Massachusetts. (War of the Coprophages)

diesel oil

Only Mulder could seriously suggest that the sludge lurking in an old crankcase was in some way paranormal. (Apocrypha)

digital tape

The only storage media known to modern science that can be displayed, read electronically, even printed, but that, for reasons unknown to modern science, can't be copied. (The Blessing Way)

digital displays

Whether on cell phones or microwave ovens, the medium for some pretty nasty messages. (Blood)

digitalis cocktail

A convenient way for eight-year-old girls to get rid of parents and other assorted adults who might cramp their wicked ways. (Eve)

dinoflagellates

These little critters so offended one of the young Eves that she suggested to a motel manager that he use chlorine to "eradicate" them from his pool. (Eve)

Discovery Channel

Great source of information on naturally occurring hallucinogenics. (Quagmire)

ditching

According to both Krycek and Scully, the worst thing someone—namely Mulder—could do to his partner. (Sleepless, Syzygy)

DNA matching

Procedure that takes weeks in the real world, mere days in the X-Files universe.

"do a Greg Louganis"

Only in the X-Filean world could a person become part of a phrase synonymous with "suicide by tying medical gauze around your neck and jumping through a window." (The Erlenmeyer Flask)

John Doe #101356

One of the least pleasant of Scully's many autopsy victims—and the only one carrying a passenger. (The Host)

dog food

What Mrs. Lowell should have had more of. (Clyde Bruckman's Final Repose)

doof!

Agent Pendrell's scathing self-commentary after flubbing and flushing in front of the lovely Agent Scully. (731)

"down the rabbit hole"

Where Lucy Householder denies going. (Oubliette)

drawstring pants

The one thing that would keep Mulder from wanting to live forever. (3)

driver's seat

Usually occupied by Mulder, the choice position is taken by Scully only a handful of times. Once just to tick him off, and once just in time to be run off the road by a psychopathic killer. Then again, she was the one to complain about Friday afternoon traffic between Atlantic City and Washington. Guess Mulder does have more experience; after all, he's already been run off the road by everything from ghosts to his own colleagues. (Syzygy, Irresistible, The Jersey Devil, Shadows, Piper Maru)

drowning

Rather unusual way to die—especially if you're sitting in the back of a police car. (Oubliette)

Druid Hill Sanitarium

While it's likely a fine psychiatric institution, the meal slots in the doors are way too big for the security of some of its inmates. (Tooms)

drunk tank

One of the better accommodations Mulder managed to find during his Big Foot safari weekend in Atlantic City. (The Jersey Devil)

dry ice

Perfect storage medium for an alien "fetus" or the head of a snooty "rocket scientist." (The Erlenmeyer Flask, Roland)

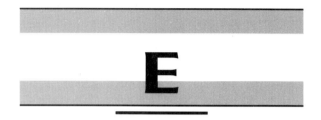

E

eight-year-olds

A dangerous age for boys in the X-Files universe, but an even more dangerous one for girls. *Boys.* **1**—Trevor Callahan dies in a vicious sandbox incident. (The Walk) **2**—Kevin Morris is declared a "threat to national security" after scribbling down the 1's and 0's he saw on his television's snowy screen. (Conduit) *Girls.* **1**—Samantha Mulder was abducted. (The X-Files: Pilot) **2**—Lucy Householder was kidnapped and held captive in a basement for five years. (Oubliette) **3**—The young Eves were kidnapped by the older Eve-6. (Eve) **4**—Michelle Bishop is possessed by the spirit of a dead man. (Born Again) **5**—Age of the progeria victim. (Young at Heart) **6**—The supposed age of Shannon Ausbury's sister when she was "sacrificed." (Die Hand Die Verletzt)

eighteen-wheeler trucks

One of numerous means of transport for Extraterrestrial Biological Entities. (E.B.E.)

Einstein

The genius that Scully dared to rewrite. Though her "Einstein's Twin Paradox: A

New Interpretation'' impressed Mulder on first reading, there's been little evidence of such continued open-mindedness since. (The X-Files: Pilot)

elevator

Otis would never have believed a simple people-mover could become so dangerous or so politically correct. (The Walk, Ghost in the Machine)

Elvis

According to Mulder, the only man ever to have successfully faked his own death. (Shadows)

"enigmatic"

Agent Scully, according to Max Fenig. (Fallen Angel)

entity rape

One of the few paranormal activities Mulder was willing to pooh-pooh—until he found himself about to drown in a bathroom. (Excelsius Dei)

evidence

Small physical proofs that have a way of not making it into—or disappearing from—secured holding areas. (almost any episode!)

evidence bag

Generic container for those oddities that won't fit in the generic sample bottle, like notes from dead men and mysterious ashes. (Young at Heart, The X-Files: Pilot)

Exeter Street

Site of the one and only occasion when an X-Filean monster returned to the scene of the crime. (Tooms, Squeeze)

exorcist

Possible occupation for Mulder if he gets turfed out of the Bureau. (The Calusari)

The Exorcist

One of Scully's favorite movies. (E.B.E.)

exsanguination

Condition afflicting cows and the fathers of Eve-9 and Eve-10. (Eve)

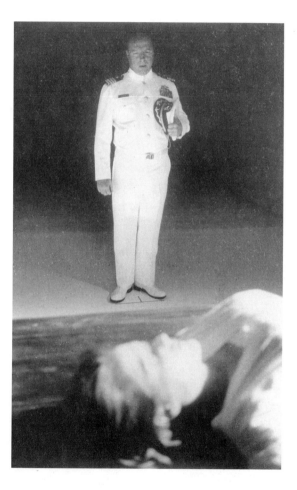

extreme possibilities

Realm into which Scully's own brief excursions tend to arise from things spiritual, such as stigmaticism and her father touching her from the grave. (Beyond the Sea)

eyeballs

Items of attention for Mrs. Paddock, Puppet, and Eve-6. Mrs. Paddock and Puppet just collected them; Eve-6 tried to eat one that was still in her guard's face. (Die Hand Die Verleztz, Clyde Bruckman's Final Repose, Eve)

eyeglasses

Worn by both agents, to the delight of audiences with a thing for "sexy intellectual types," but only Mulder has used his to sneak out evidence right under the noses of CIA operatives. (Shadows)

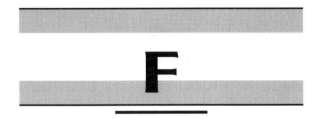

F

FBI Training Academy

According to the mother of Scully's god-son, the perfect preparation for parent-hood. (The Jersey Devil)

FBI's Most Unwanted

Mulder. (The X-Files: Pilot)

fallen angel

An "official" code name for the officially nonexistent objects that the average lay-man might otherwise recognize as UFOs. (Fallen Angel)

family members

The X-Filean version of *Star Trek*'s red-shirted security officers.

"fat, little, white, Nazi storm trooper"

Bruckman's eerily accurate description of a propane tank at Glenview Lake. (Clyde Bruckman's Final Repose)

fathers

Characters that get more airtime posthumously than they did while they were alive! (One Breath, Talitha Cumi, The Blessing Way, Beyond the Sea, etc.)

FBI tour

The way ex-agents get back into the J. Edgar Hoover Building. (The Blessing Way)

February 23

Scully's birthday, or not. (Lazarus, 731)

"the fence"

Not a length of rails and palings, but a highly sophisticated border reaching out into space—a barrier that can be broken only by jets, missiles, meteors . . . or UFOs. (Fallen Angel)

Max Fenig

Holds the distinction of being the *second* person Mulder believes he lost to aliens. (Fallen Angel)

"fifth- and sixth-degree burns"

Though most medical personnel have never heard of anything above a third-degree burn, Scully has encountered them *twice*. Once when a "fallen angel" irradiated a bunch of unsuspecting soldiers, and again when Cecil L'Ively became the human torch. (Fallen Angel, Fire, Piper Maru, Apocrypha)

fifth floor

Place in FBI Headquarters that is as far from Mulder's basement office, both physically and morally, as possible.

fingerprints

A handy forensic tool—if the fingerprints in question aren't ten inches long, or suggest your suspect is over a hundred years old. (Squeeze)

film noir

Cinematic style that not only provides mood and atmosphere, but hides off-screen pregnancies and keeps the audience wondering how much of the action occurs first in their own imaginations.

firecrackers

Capable of making even seasoned agents jumpy. (Hell Money)

first-class airfare
How the crooks get to travel while Mulder squirms in coach. (Piper Maru)

fishtanks
Never what they appear in the X-Files universe. Who could imagine a full-grown man *drowning* in one? Then there's the tank in Mulder's apartment—it doesn't have any fish! The tanks found on Pan- dora Street, on the other hand, hold exactly one alien-gene-altered human per tank. (Born Again, The Erlenmeyer Flask, Little Green Men)

flaking skin
First sign that your date isn't what he appears to be, especially if he smells like dish detergent. (2SHY)

flash-frozen

The government's preferred method of storing unacknowledged alien tissue. (The Erlenmeyer Flask)

flashlights

The $4,000 prop every real X-Phile wants to have. They come in two handy-dandy sizes, one for the trunk, one for the handbag.

"a faint floral odor"

In perfume, Scully might have appreciated that little touch; in a cadaver, it disturbed her on a number of levels. (Revelations)

Flying Saucer Diner

Where you can get a decent cup of coffee for 50 cents and evidence of UFO technology for a mere $20 more. (Deep Throat)

fog

Convenient adjunct to the film noir style.

fool's errand

How Mulder and Scully define any case not immediately and directly bearing on their own interests. Used interchangeably with wild-goose chase. (The Host, Our Town, etc.)

football

The obsession of *The X-Files* writing team, the sport was featured in more than a dozen episodes and even made it into the credits. (Die Hand Die Verletzt)

Forty-sixth Street, New York City

Meeting place for the Consortium and the Cigarette-Smoking Man's home away from home. (The Blessing Way)

four-leaf clover

Unluckiest "lucky" charm in the history of the 'Files. Instead of "getting lucky," Lauren MacKalvey got ingested by her date. (2SHY)

"four-bagger"

The censure-transfer-suspension-probation home run that Skinner was convinced would lead to Mulder's expulsion from the Bureau. (Little Green Men)

foxglove

The deadly plant that both Cindy and Teena cultivated, distilled, and fed to their fathers. (Eve)

"Free James Brown" rallies

Where Frohike spends his off-hours. (Fearful Symmetry)

Friday the 13th (April)

More than a little unlucky for William Mulder, nearly as unlucky for Dana Scully. (Anasazi)

frogs

Chester Bonaparte earned 50 cents for each one he caught; Scully had them falling at her feet for free! (Fresh Bones, Die Hand Die Verletzt)

Frohike

The paranoid Lone Gunman who describes Scully as "tasty" and Mulder as "a redwood among sprouts."

"full circle"

Where Scully goes to find her own truths. (Revelations)

"full denial"

The blank wall that the investigative duo of Mulder and Scully so frequently find themselves up against, or the personal state Mulder assumes most by-the-book agents already suffer from. (Shadows)

"full of it"

How Assistant Special Agent in Charge Reggie Purdue described a young Fox Mulder. (Young at Heart)

funeral wreaths

Donny Pfaster's idea of bedroom accessories. (Irresistible)

furry vests

Only Frohike could honestly consider one of these the ultimate in fashion statements. (Nisei)

G

gargoyle

The X-Filean version pro-vided writers with a unique place to hide body parts, at least when they weren't busy animating the things and letting them attack beleaguered federal agents. (Grotesque)

garnet

If the guys chasing you are wearing this color beret, run faster. (Little Green Men)

general assignment

Luckily for the victims of fat-sucking and other assorted monsters, general assignment cases are handled by someone other than the Daring Duo. The high mortality rate among agents, such as Jerry Lamana, who accidentally find themselves involved in X-Files suggests Mulder and Scully probably know better. (Ghost in the Machine)

General Mutual Life Insurance Policy

The bribe Mulder used on Clyde Bruckman to get him to examine a piece of evidence "psychically." (Clyde Bruckman's Final Repose)

genetic mutation

Damn good explanation for all things X-Filean that refuse to follow the known precepts of science.

Gertie's

Washington pub where Mulder offers Scully a drink before Happy Hour and where Deep Throat conducts secret meetings with federal agents in the john. Deep Throat once actually sat at a table. (Deep Throat, Young at Heart)

get-well presents

As Scully recovered from her brush with death, Mulder turned up with a football video and the tiny gold cross last seen in Duane Barry's trunk. It was the scruffy Frohike who came bearing flowers. (One Breath)

girlie scream

The scream that was only described in "War of the Coprophages" comes to life, sort of, in "Jose Chung's 'From Outer Space.'"

glossolalia

A condition that leaves its victims muttering incoherently and X-Philes rummaging through their dictionaries. (Oubliette)

"grande 2 percent cappuccino with vanilla"

The vital item that Agent Kazdan thought Krycek just might be capable of procuring for her. (Duane Barry)

grave-digging

A pleasure Scully'd never had—until she started working with Mulder. She found it even less pleasant after meeting Donnie Pfaster, who'd made it into his nocturnal hobby. (The X-Files: Pilot, Irresistible)

Howard Graves

As a result of continuity errors, the only man on *The X-Files* to die on two different dates—two weeks apart—and still be an active participant in all the posthumous action! Viewers, however, could be forgiven for thinking they were dealing with two different men. Thanks again to the prop department, Graves has two different names as well. A newspaper article lists him as Howard Thomas Graves, but his headstone dubs him Howard Patrick Graves. (Shadows)

"the gray suit"

Mulder's second wardrobe choice for the Tooms psychiatric review. (Tooms)

"great seats"

What Mulder suspects Deep Throat would be capable of procuring—along with, from time to time, a little alien DNA. (E.B.E.)

green bottle fly
Only on *The X-Files* could a common household insect become a murder suspect. (The List)

green goo
Olive oil? Snake oil? The odd substance Mulder thinks is alien blood. (Nisei)

gross-out scene
Deliberately written into each and every X-Filean script, the GOS has the nasty habit of involving BOWs.

grotesque
Only an X-Filean artist could take a naked-as-you're-going-to-get-on-TV hunk and make him *that* ugly. (Grotesque)

Gulf War Syndrome
Handy excuses for the odd behavior of men like Colonel Buddahas and Lieutenant Colonel Stans. (Deep Throat, The Walk)

gun
Item Mulder rarely fires—but frequently loses! Scully's track record is considerably better; she generally hits whatever she's aiming at—even her bullheaded partner—and is more likely to have her gun handy when needed.

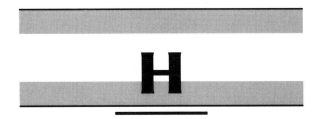

H

hagiographic fabrications

Mulder's description of the Bible. (Revelations)

haiku

Tongue-in-cheek reference to the notes that murderer John Barnett sent to Mulder. (Young at Heart)

George Ellery Hale

Real-life founder of the Palomar Observatory who just happened to think he'd been visited by elves. Not surprisingly, it's also one of Mulder's pseudonyms. (Little Green Men)

handy-dandy trunk kit

Spray paint, Geiger counters, stopwatches, evidence bags, surgical gloves, mega-wattage flashlights in two convenient sizes, a compass, and a variety of probes, all wrapped up in a trunk-sized suitcase that allows Mulder instant access to his alien-tracking gear. (The X-Files: Pilot)

Hanky Panky
magazine

One of Mulder's more unusual sources for locating women who claim to have been held in "anti-gravity chambers" aboard UFOs. (The Jersey Devil)

hard bargaining

The only practical option for a scientist carrying around information the "shadow" government wants. (Ghost in the Machine)

"Have a really nice day"
Perky answering machine message re-corded by Melissa Scully. (The Blessing Way)

Havez
Both a cop with a belief in the Stupendous Yappi's ability and an allusion to the real Jean Havez, who worked with the real Clyde Bruckman. (Clyde Bruckman's Final Repose)

health class
The one subject Darren Oswald claims to have excelled in. (D.P.O.)

Heinrich
The Norwegian elkhound Mulder wished he'd really had when he caught up with a certain mutant under an escalator. (Tooms)

hell money
A useful currency to carry if you're inves-tigating involuntary organ donation in Chinatown. (Hell Money)

Jimi Hendrix
The man Mulder wanted Luther Lee Boggs to "channel" so he could catch an-other rendition of "All Along the Watch-tower." (Beyond the Sea)

"high-capacity, compact weapon"
X's favorite means of persuasion. (One Breath)

"high-ranking diplomat"
Secret agent–speak for "spy who got caught on someone else's turf." (Nisei)

highway hypnosis
What Mulder gets from "Big Blue's" ap-petites. (Quagmire)

"hokey"

Term used to describe the alien autopsy aired not once, but twice, on the Fox-TV network. (Nisei)

homemade bread

Not a menu recommendation if you happen to be invited to Kristin Kilar's house. (3)

"Homer Simpson's evil twin"

The incredibly accurate—and conveniently self-promoting—description of Kevin Kreider's "guardian angel." (Revelations)

Home Value Network

Proof that TV is dangerous to your pocketbook as well as to your mental health. (Wetwired)

Hong Kong

Unlikely destination to be covered by the Bureau's travel expenses section. (Piper Maru)

hornéd beasts

When Mulder and Detective White claim to see one burnt into a young man's chest, Scully steadfastly refuses to exhibit the slightest degree of imagination. (Syzygy)

"Hot!"

How Frohicke of the Lone Gunmen describes Scully, and how millions of fans think of Gillian Anderson. (E.B.E.)

Lucy Householder

One of only two women that Special Agent Fox Mulder has ever cried over. (Oubliette, Conduit)

"hung like a club-tailed dragonfly"

One gets the impression that Mulder rather wished Dr. Bambi was talking about him instead of a mechanical bug. (War of the Coprophages)

"hurt you like that beastwoman"

Scully's promise to Mulder if he doesn't butt out of her personal life. (The Jersey Devil)

hydrotherapy

Takes on a whole new meaning when Lieutenant Colonel Stans throws himself into a tub of boiling water. (The Walk)

hypnosis

Whether for convulsions or memory loss, Mulder's preferred method of treatment. Even Scully gives it a whirl—once. As Mulder's own repressed memories, dug up from the black hole of his experiences of the night Samantha disappeared, vary considerably from his dreams and the facts as he knows them, it's questionable if even he depends on it unreservedly.

"I got hit by a car"
One of the better reasons Mulder has managed to come up with for not filing regular, standardized reports. (Colony)

"I just knew"
The less-than-completely-scientific reason Scully gives for her certainty that her partner was still alive.

"I only get five?"
Scully's woeful response to Mulder's question about which five people she'd choose to exact her revenge on if she could come back from the dead. (The List)

"I want to believe!"
Oft-expressed sentiment of Fox Mulder—though what exactly he wants to believe in seems to vary with each episode.

ice cream
Scully's favorite dessert or midnight snack. (Duane Barry, War of the Cropophages)

ice-fishing
Scully's idea of a fun date. (Lazarus)

iced tea
The drink that might have brought Mulder and Scully together. She brought root beer instead. (Tooms)

Immelman
An aerial maneuver intended to confound an Air Force colonel who once performed it with ease. (Deep Throat)

"impertinent questions"
According to Mulder, the path to pertinent answers. (The X-Files: Pilot)

implants
The *de rigueur* accessory for all abductees. Not advised for use with your grocery store variety of price scanners. (Duane Barry)

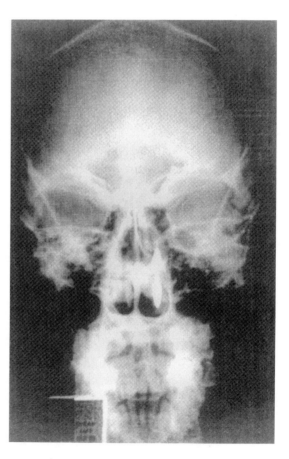

incident on the rock
When Mulder and Scully are "stranded" on a rock in Heuvelman's Lake, romantics everywhere began dreaming of a more intimate relationship for the Dynamic Duo. (Quagmire)

innocently by-standing agent
The pose that Mulder and Scully, decked out in carbon-copy trenchcoats while behind the wheels of government-issue rental cars, have never been able to carry off during stakeouts.

"insanity"
The only sane response to an insane world. (The Walk)

"the intelligence community"
A neighborhood that Skinner would just as soon not move to. (Piper Maru)

interpreter
Hard thing to find in Allentown, Pennsylvania, at least at three in the morning. (Nisei)

iron depletion
A chronic condition of the residents of the Reticuli systems, it's commonly believed by those in the know to be responsible for their pale gray skin tones and their taste for terrestrial livers. (Squeeze, Tooms)

Iron Maiden
What Nancy Spiller, one of Scully's instructors (but not the one she was dating), was called behind her back. (Squeeze)

J

J.A.S.D. Beef Company

There's no Mad Cow Disease in sight, but, of the three men Scully is known to have shot during her career, one died here, and something much more insidious infected the employees' children. (Red Museum)

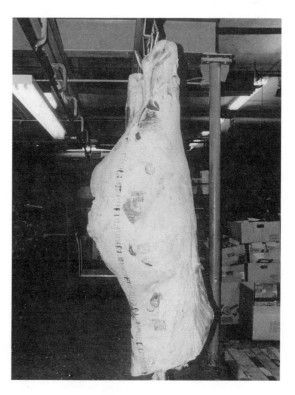

Japanese

Language Mulder wishes he had studied instead of French. (731)

Owen Jarvis

According to Mrs. Kreider, a passable gardener; according to kids at a local shelter, the Devil; according to Mulder, a suspect in a kidnapping; according to Scully, a saint in the making. (Revelations)

"Jerk!"

One of the many ways Scully has described Mulder to her girl chums, along with "cute" and "obsessed." (The Jersey Devil)

Jersey Devil

According to Mulder, a candidate for the next Miss USA competition—despite her rather odd diet.

Jesus Christ: Superstar

Ironically inappropriate dramatic production that was vetoed at Crowley High School. (Die Hand Die Verletzt)

Carl Gustav Jung

Though Mulder frequently "forgets" he's an Oxford-trained psychologist—and never mentions an area of specialization—he often quotes Jung, who, in addition to his theory of the collective unconscious, also wrote on the possibility of aliens visiting Earth on a regular basis. Right up Mulder's alley. (Aubrey)

jurisdiction

Totally ignored facet of an X-Files investigation.

justice

A holy grail likely to lead its pursuers into ethical dilemmas no blind statue could have anticipated.

K

"a kind three"

Where Brother Martin's last "date" ranked him/her on a scale of ten. (GenderBender)

Kindred

If the Addams Family got religion, they'd be almost as scary as the sexually confused Kindred. (GenderBender)

Kline

Minnesota cop who listened intently to the Stupendous Yappi's description of the tea-reader's death throes, less intently to Mulder's more prosaic performance. Also an allusion to yet another of the real-life Clyde Bruckman's associates. (Clyde Bruckman's Final Repose)

"a knack for pissing people off"

What New Age priests tend to have in the X-Files universe. (Red Museum)

Kristin Kilar

Only woman we've seen Mulder "get lucky" with. (3)

Karen Kosseff

A social worker whose caseload includes agents who may or may not have been abducted by aliens or some shadow government, as well as little boys who hiss, spit, and cause the paint to peel off nearby walls. (Irresistible, The Calusari)

Kevin Kreider

While the staff of *The X-Files* was busy recycling the K.K. initials so popular among guest characters, the character himself was nearly recycled at the 21st Century Recycling Plant in Jerusalem, Ohio. (Revelations)

Alex Krycek

Patsy or principal player? Though accused of several crimes, among them causing the death of William Mulder, no one has ever *seen* him do more than pistol-whip a skytram operator. His assignment as Mulder's partner was undoubtedly arranged at a higher level of power, though it often appeared he was as unsure of his ultimate function as his new partner was of him.

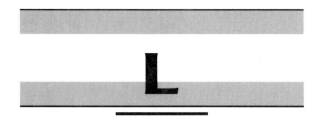

"La Lucky Charm"

Although Mulder forked over the $5 for Chester's, Scully would eventually prove that it was a bit more useful than the fuzzy dice she'd originally compared it to. (Fresh Bones)

lady in red

Takes on a whole new meaning with the Little Red Riding Hood in question, who likes to appear in mirrors and nightmares just to scream her head off and then disappear. (Avatar)

lady's fingers

The ones found in Donny Pfaster's freezer wouldn't appeal to many tastes—they still sport bright red nail polish. (Irresistible)

Langly

The Lone Gunman who has a philosophical problem with the notion of his picture being bounced off a satellite. (Fearful Symmetry)

Lariat

The rental company that continues to hand out cars to Mulder and Scully even though both agents have a habit of wrecking their vehicles. (Piper Maru, Irresistible, etc.)

late-industrial-welding

The decor style favored by the patrons of Club Tepes. (3)

"the latex"

See prophylactic. (Syzygy)

Lichfield

Day-care center for the eugenically challenged. (Eve)

light switch

The last thing Scully or Mulder seem inclined to use on entering dark rooms—even rooms with four hundred pounds of rampaging gorilla in them! (Fearful Symmetry)

lightning

One of Connorville's local products. It *does* strike twice—and more!—in the X-Files universe. (D.P.O.)

lightning rod

Yet another career opportunity for Darren Oswald. (D.P.O.)

list

It's not healthy to be on any list featured in an X-File, particularly not any lists kept by Neetch Manly. (The List)

"a little drool"

Nothing between friends. (Pusher)

"little green men"

According to Mulder, that's a misnomer, they're actually "little gray men." (Squeeze)

liver

Sauteed, and with a few onions on the side, the favorite dish of Reticulans. Incredibly rare, with absolutely no condiments, the favorite dish of Eugene Victor Tooms. (Squeeze, Tooms)

liverwurst
Stakeout munchie. (Tooms)

locusts
Either a sign of divine intervention or proof that potato skins attract bugs. (Miracle Man)

The Lone Gunman
A magazine topped only by *Adult Video News* and *Celebrity Skin* on Mulder's must-read list.

Lone Gunmen
Great guys to know if you need a security pass in a hurry, or a pair of night-vision goggles, even a copy of some top-secret government files. They are not, however, the guys you want on your covert stakeout and recovery missions. (E.B.E., Anasazi, Apocrypha)

Lonely Hearts
The supposedly desperate people who frequent the personal ads and computer bulletin boards in search of Mr. or Miss Right. (2SHY)

The Look
Scully's usual first response to her partner's wilder notions, The Look can be modified by any one or combination of deep sighs, raised eyebrows, or eye rolls, but is not to be confused with The Tender Look or The Significant Look.

Looney Tunes

Gets a thumbs-down from the young Eves. They preferred to not only watch but tape the presidential address. (Eve)

lost time

1—Disconcertingly frequent occurrence that's cost Scully and Mulder over three months' worth of memories in their three years as partners; including nine minutes each in The X-Files Pilot. **2**—Alternately, the disconcerting feeling experienced by viewers as they realize that the internal X-Filean timeline has placed our intrepid heroes in two different locations on the same dates; or that it takes Mulder nearly as long to drive directly to a crime scene as it takes Scully to assist a victim, wait for the ambulance, accompany the victim to the hospital, accompany the victim back to a police station, make a report, argue with the chief of police, and, after locating a new car, drive herself to the same scene. (Fallen Angel, Aubrey)

lottery tickets

Something you'd like to buy if you were *behind* Clyde Bruckman in the line. (Clyde Bruckman's Final Repose)

love lives

What neither Mulder nor Scully seems to have. Maybe Skinner will have better luck.

low-fat milk

What not to offer Virgil Incanto. (2SHY)

F.M. Luder

The pseudonym under which Mulder published an article on the Gulf Breeze sightings in *Omni*. (Fallen Angel)

M

maggots

Made guest appearances, necessitating the hiring of a Maggot Wrangler. (The List, Fresh Bones)

maid's day off

Fictional cause for the frequent disarray in Mulder's apartment. (Nisei)

mailman

You wouldn't *really* want to have Rappo's mailman delivering anything to your house. (The Walk)

mango-kiwi-tropical swirl

On finding this unusual—and sickly—flavor in Pusher's fridge, Mulder had the last piece of evidence he needed to assure himself that Pusher was indeed a little mad. (Pusher)

manicures

These get grisly on *The X-Files*. To retrieve a wedding band, ''Jack Willis'' took a set of surgical shears to Warren Dupree's fingers. Donnie Pfaster kept the fingers of his victims instead. (Lazarus, Irresistible)

manila envelopes

The natural habitat for information that has been "liberated" from its proper home in filing cabinets somewhere under the Pentagon, in mountain vaults, or in the hidden recesses of the Lone Gunmen's offices.

Marty Mulder

Yet another of Mulder's aliases. (3)

masking tape

Mulder's way of avoiding phone and telegram bills. (Deep Throat)

mass graves

The Dynamic Duo couldn't find them in "Syzygy," but Scully almost ends up in one during "731."

math

As evidenced by his calculations in the episode "Lazarus," not Mulder's strong suit.

Richard Matheson

Senator with a serious case of on-again, off-again ethics.

Dr. Mengele

The not-so-friendly name given Dr. Joseph Ridley by his peers before he was refused membership in the American Medical Association. (Young at Heart)

metal detector

Surefire way to detect the presence of previously unsuspected microchip implants. Also occasionally useful at airports. (The Blessing Way, Revelations, Piper Maru, Colony)

metallic implants

The pesky bits of evidence that have a habit of turning up unexpectedly in a variety of body cavities. The Cigarette-Smoking Man has his own personal collection secreted away in the Pentagon basement, though the Allentown chapter of MUFON has been amassing a sizable collection of its own. (The X-Files: Pilot, Nisei)

meteor

In the X-Files universe, these are known to "hover" over small midwestern towns. (Fallen Angel)

Mexican standoff

Tarantino move over—*The X-Files* has the peculiar distinction of being the only program to have featured a *three-way* Mexican standoff, between Scully, Mulder, and Skinner. (Paper Clip)

MIB (Men in Black)

A mysterious band of men who spend their time warning people not to discuss their UFO-related experiences; some are also known to bear an uncanny resemblance to Alex Trebek. (Jose Chung's "From Outer Space")

Miller's Grove

Like the Grover's Mill of *War of the Worlds*, an unlikely place for an alien invasion. (War of the Coprophages)

"millstone of humiliation"

What Mulder is willing to endure to pull the chains of both the gullible and the skeptical. (Squeeze)

Military

1—Installations. The sites of suspicious activities. **2**—Personnel. Inherently suspicious people. **3**—Psychiatrist. Unlikely to believe even a colonel who claims some mysterious force "won't let me die!" (The Walk) **4**—Files. Generally incomplete, except for those occasions when they include amputated chicken feet. (The Walk, Fresh Bones)

mind game player extraordinaire

How Mulder describes his former flame, Scotland Yard Inspector Phoebe Green. (Fire)

miner's cap

Mulder's father, despite his connection to the Strughold Mine, never came home with a light attached to the front of his hat. (Paper Clip)

miracles

Though Mulder is the "believer," it's Scully who is the only one to verbally profess a belief in the existence and power of miracles. (Revelations)

Mr. Congeniality

How Mulder describes himself in response to Scully's concerns that he was "antagonizing local law enforcement." (Conduit)

MJ Files

AKA the Majestic Files, not something you'd like to mention aloud in the X-Files universe—unless you *like* having strange men in ski masks rummaging through your underwear and computer files. (Anasazi)

monkey-pee

What Scully didn't find in an Erlenmeyer Flask. (The Erlenmeyer Flask)

monkey-wrenchers

In the real world, extreme environmentalists; in the X-Filean world, second course for glowing green bugs with a taste for flannel. (Darkness Falls)

morphing

Among the favorite SFX of the X-crew—second only to flying on the list of things to "work in"—it's more than an affordable "trick" now that it's been associated with Mulder's first, best link to his missing sister. (The X-Files: Pilot)

mosquito bites

The only thing—so far!—to send Scully running half-naked into Mulder's arms. (The X-Files: Pilot)

moving violation

Reason enough for a man to be chased by two black-and-whites, beaten, jolted with a tazer, shot twice, and run off the end of a wharf into a harbor. (The Erlenmeyer Flask)

Mrs. Spooky

According to one of Scully's classmates, her fate if she remains immersed in the X-Files. (Squeeze)

Special Agent Fox Mulder

A curious mix of cynic and believer, Fox Mulder remains convinced that his only sister, Samantha, was abducted by aliens when they were children. That belief, the driving force of his adult life, has led him to investigate all manner of paranormal events in his search for the Truth.

Trained as a psychologist at Oxford (though his knowledge of the field often seems to come up short when Scully spouts off about her latest pet syndrome), he distinguished himself in the Violent Crimes Section as a criminal profiler. Despite that early success, he requested a permanent assignment to the X-Files after he stumbled across them some years later. That request was granted, at least in part, because of the influence of Mulder's acquaintances "on the Hill," an influence he may have inherited from his father, who once worked for the State Department.

The three years he and Scully have spent investigating the X-Files have brought him close to some tantalizing Truths, so close he may now be willing to sacrifice everything he's accomplished for just one more Answer. In many ways, Mulder is his own worst enemy, his own Achilles' heel.

Mulder's bedroom

One of the yet unexplained mysteries of the X-Files universe. Where is it?

Mulder salad

Found in Navajo hogans. (The Blessing Way)

murder weapons

Who needs knives and guns when you've got electrically retracting bleachers and garage-door springs to hand? (Syzygy)

mushrooms

More than a pizza topping at the Excelsius Dei Convalescent Home. (Excelsius Dei)

Mutual UFO Network

Support and information group whose members have a unique form of membership card—a bottle containing "implants" removed from their necks.

The Mystery of the Horny Beast

What Scully found her partner and Detective White trying to solve late one night in Mulder's motel room. (Syzygy)

N

Napier's Constant

The "key" given to Mulder and Scully by Victor Klemper that allows them access to a literal mountain of information. (Paper Clip)

nasal cavities

According to witnesses, one of the favorite storage spaces for metallic implants. (The X-Files: Pilot)

Navajo

Good people to find if you've been shot. Good people to know if you've got coded WWII documents to be deciphered. Bad people to double-cross. (Anasazi, The Blessing Way, Paper Clip)

hogan, Navajo

Place to find a Mulder salad, hold an Old Boys' Club reunion for the mortality-challenged, or get paid your usual $100,000 an episode for eight lines and a long nap. (The Blessing Way)

neck scars

After encountering Darren Peter Oswald and Augustus Cole, a feature Mulder and Scully should automatically consider highly suspicious. (D.P.O., Sleepless)

need-to-know basis

Though Mulder often accuses both his superiors and his sources of rationing out information in dribs and drabs, he, in turn, frequently leaves his partner in the dark until he's already dragged her off to some remote location. (Hell Money, Quagmire, etc.)

"new life form"

The notation you *don't* want to find scribbled across case notes while you're investigating a serial murder at a remote volcanic study camp. (Firewalker)

New York Knicks T-shirt

Bruckman thought something was one when it wasn't, Dupree thought something wasn't one when it was. (Clyde Bruckman's Final Repose, Beyond the Sea)

NICAP

According to Max Fenig, an offshoot of the Fox Mulder Appreciation Society. In addition to chasing down UFOs, its members have been known to ransack the rooms of traveling federal agents. (Fallen Angel)

NICAP cap

Mulder's last memento of the missing Max Fenig, it makes another appearance later. (Fallen Angel, Beyond the Sea)

"nice trip to the forest"

An offer Scully should never have taken Mulder up on. (Darkness Falls)

night-vision goggles

What Mulder got from Frohike in return for Scully's home number. (Blood)

ninja party

How Kenneth Soona (AKA the Thinker) describes the agents "shagging" his butt. (Anasazi)

Nisei

First generation Japanese-Americans. (Nisei)

"Nobody's gonna spoil us"

Something you don't want to hear your daughter murmuring in her sleep. (Oubliette)

Norwegian cocktail

Take the juice of six lemons, add the squeezings from a can of sardines, and top with the fluid from a snow globe. (Død Kalm)

nosebleeds

An obvious sign of a victim's involvement in the paranormal, just ask Peggy O'Dell, Lucy Householder, or Max Fenig. Guess the moral is: If a great SFX prosthetic works once . . . (The X-Files: Pilot, Oubliette, Fallen Angel)

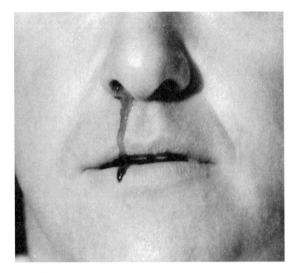

Obi-Wan Kenobi crap

Mulder's description of his relationship with Deep Throat. (The Erlenmeyer Flask)

"off the record"

Where all the best information lurks. (GenderBender)

Office of Professional Conduct

That section of the Justice Department most likely to issue "mandatory leave" to Mulder or Scully at least once per season.

"official"

A direct contradiction of anything resembling Mulder's Truth.

Okobogee

Campground for aliens and humans alike, both have been visiting there for generations to enjoy the great "fishing." (Conduit)

old-growth trees

Better left alone unless you've got several flashlights, a lot of spare batteries, and a really big bug-zapper. (Darkness Falls)

old-fashioned

Another word for sexist. (2SHY)

"ONE"

Along with naked, what neither "HE" nor "SHE" wanted to be in Delta Glen, Wisconsin. (Red Museum)

opera

Site of X's best naps. (End Game)

Operation Falcon

Covert name for the UFO hunters who don't officially exist (Fallen Angel)

orangutan
A convenient label for corpses that, while clearly not human, Scully might not wish to admit are a tad . . . unearthly. (The X-Files: Pilot)

orchid
A flower Scully is unlikely to appreciate after her encounters with that orchid aficionado, Victor Klemper. (Paper Clip)

organ donation
Popular among X-Filean guest characters like Howard Graves, who conveniently left bits and pieces of evidence lying about in other people's bodies, it proved less attractive to the Chinese community. (Shadows, Hell Money)

origami figures
What you don't want to find on your front doorstep if Michelle Bishop lives in your neighborhood. (Born Again)

"orthodox procedure"
What the brass wanted, but didn't get. (Tooms)

Darren Peter Oswald
With his sizzling personality, he could have put the Energizer Bunny out of business. (D.P.O.)

"out there"
Along with the elusive Truth, lots of things have been "out there" since *The X-Files* debuted three years ago. While Samantha, aliens, and UFOs seem content to hover just out of reach, one or two other things have arrived from "out there" —often with terrifying results. Martian faces, Arctic ice worms, and "fallen angels" have all conspired to keep Mulder's faith in the immensity of all things "out there." (Space, Ice, Fallen Angel)

Ovaltine Diner
Place to get good sweet-potato pie and the occasional answer. (Jose Chung's "From Outer Space")

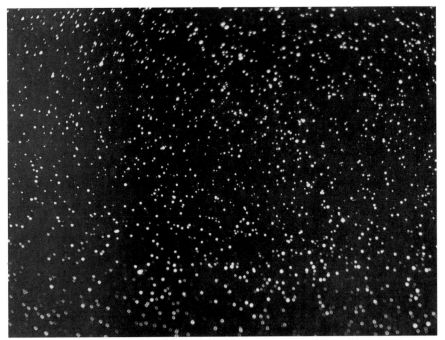

ovaries

According to Mulder, items of considerable interest to alien abductors. (Duane Barry)

Oxford

Where Phoebe Green claims Mulder left his sense of humor. (Fire)

oxygen cyanide M-43 grenade

What would, in this "green" era, come with a "Not To Be Used in Enclosed Boxcar" warning. (The Blessing Way)

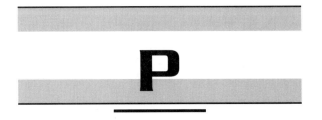

P

Mrs. Phyllis H. Paddock
The original "teacher from hell." (Die Hand Die Verletzt)

paint cans
Convenient storage for severed heads. (The List)

painted desert
Takes on a whole new interpretation when the X-crew sprays a gravel pit outside Vancouver. (Anasazi, The Blessing Way)

Paper Clip
Name given to the American operation that saw dozens of Germany's top scientists, most of whom were about to be legitimately charged with war crimes, brought secretly into the United States. (Paper Clip)

paper cut
The innocuous little injury that leads an X-Filean postal employee into a life of crime. (Blood)

papier-mâché

"Hobby" for Eugene Victor Tooms. (Tooms)

parking

Viewers could begin to think the X-crew had a thing against the all-American sport of parking with your date on a Saturday night. Elizabeth Hawley and James Summers were yanked from their gently rocking vehicle by serial killer Henry Lucas. Lauren was attacked by her date, the fat-sucking Virgil Incanto. "Brother" Martin's date never was sure just who he'd invited into his car—but the experience likely turned him off parking for some time. (Beyond the Sea, 2SHY, GenderBender)

parking spots

Clyde Bruckman can really pick 'em. (Clyde Bruckman's Final Repose)

Special Agent Bill Patterson

One of Mulder's early mentors, but hardly one of his idols. (Grotesque)

pearl diving

What a certain Japanese "diplomat" probably wasn't doing in a local canal. (Nisei)

pencil

A portable, efficient, scientific instrument that requires no power source, but is capable of bringing up latent images from brown paper packaging. (Apocrypha)

pets

Short-lived creatures in the X-Filean world. (Syzygy, Quagmire, Teso dos Bichos, etc.)

phantom soldier

A "Flying Dutchman" for the nineties. (The Walk)

phosphorescent lipstick

What Carina Sayles must have been wearing if you don't buy into the "apparition in red" theory. (Avatar)

"pig!"

How Mulder's only known date described him. (Little Green Men)

pie (coconut cream, lemon meringue, or banana cream)

It obsessed Clyde Bruckman; Mulder stepped in it; a serial killer nearly turned it to his own advantage. (Clyde Bruckman's Final Repose)

pillowcases
Convenient substitutes for the traditional black hood when your execution is in a less than traditional location, like a bedroom. (Nisei)

pine
The car scent Mulder prefers to use when the burger containers build up on the seat during a stakeout. (Tooms)

"plausible denial"
Secret agent–Speak for what every good covert agent wants for Christmas. (Anasazi)

plumber's snake
Along with a toddler-proof lid closure, an effective defense against Eugene Tooms. (Tooms)

Dr. Mark Pomerantz
Specialist in the fields of psychotherapy, hypnotic regression, energy fields, and scaring the life out of female FBI agents by coming a little too close to the truth. Also a good friend of Melissa Scully. (The Blessing Way)

post-traumatic stress syndrome
Scully's pat answer when "bipolar disorder" doesn't seem to fit the bill. (The Walk, Deep Throat, Firewalker, etc.)

potato
One of the many things Scully and Mulder have exhumed. Whether it's the weirdest or most normal item is still up for debate. (Humbug)

power-suiting
Scully's standard garb for the office and street chases alike.

"a praying mantis epiphany"
The innocuous little bug that led to Mulder's first "girlie scream." (War of the Coprophages)

"pretty temporary"
Most things in Lucy Householder's brief life. (Oubliette)

prisons
In the X-Files universe, bad places to come down with "'flu-like symptoms," keep your family album on the wall, or start writing up lists of those who've been naughty or nice. (F. Emasculata, Eve, The List)

progeria
This disease, which usually makes the young old, made John Barnett young again. (Young at Heart)

"proper channels"
What Mulder and Scully veer from with predictable regularity. (Firewalker)

prophylactic
Nothing sexual here, just Mulder's pet name for the multitude of latex surgical gloves that Scully always seems to have in some pocket or other. (Soft Light)

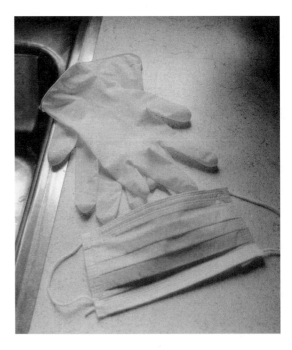

Puerto Rico

Especially around Arecibo's SETI installations, good hunting grounds for aliens and AWOL agents. (Little Green Men)

pulling a Darth Vader

What fans began to dread might happen when the cozy chats between the Cigarette-Smoking Man and Mulder's mother suggested to some that Mulder's nemesis might be more than a "friend of the family." (Talitha Cumi)

purity control

Password or monkey-pee? Either way, it was up to Scully to use it. Neither pure nor controlled, it would resurface later. (The Erlenmeyer Flask, Red Museum)

quarantine

The periods during which, rather than stay confined to their allotted hospital beds, our heroes solve seven more cases. (Darkness Falls, Ice)

Queequag

Named for the cannibal from *Moby Dick,* Scully's dog—the one that ate its original owner. It was itself eaten as a result of yet another of Mulder's monster chases. (Clyde Bruckman's Final Repose, Quagmire)

Quinnimount, West Virginia

Where Mulder plans to catch a train hobo-style. (Nisei)

Quonochontaug

The unpronounceable (for Skinner at least) name of the community where the Mulders kept a summer home and where Mrs. Mulder, years later, kept an appointment with a water-skiing smoker. (Talitha Cumi)

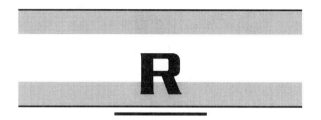

Rat-Tail Productions

Distributors for a genuine, guaranteed video of an alien autopsy. (Nisei)

"really delicate work"

Mulder's summation of the NSA's search technique, made as he picked up the pieces of a broken piggy bank. (Conduit)

Reclamations

Euphemism for the mad scramble to recover the remains of "nonexistent" flying saucers and their equally "imaginary" pilots. (Fallen Angel)

rectal thermometer

The complex piece of medical equipment that so stumped a school nurse and *Dr. Scully* that it eventually found its way into Kevin Kreider's *mouth*! (Revelations)

red-green color blindness

The genetic condition that Mulder managed to hide or ignore for all but one episode of *The X-Files*'s first three seasons. (Wetwired)

regression hypnosis

For Mulder, confirmation; for Scully, confusion. (Nisei)

reincarnation

Very popular philosophical belief on death row. (The List)

"remotely plausible"

How Mulder rates the chances that someone would find his partner attractive. (E.B.E.)

retroviruses

Used when the good old post-traumatic stress syndrome or bipolar condition can't explain a mysterious death or the onset of bizarre behavior. (End Game)

right field

While most of his ideas were out in left field, Mulder played right field as a Little Leaguer. (Blood)

Rob

The one and only man to get Scully out of her power suits on screen. However, he failed to hold her attention that evening and even Cirque d'Soleil tickets couldn't lure her out of her self-imposed solitude. (The Jersey Devil)

Russian roulette

Pusher's favorite afternoon entertainment. (Pusher)

S

salamanders

Part of the genetic soup from which Dr. Ridley grew a new hand for John Barnett. (Young at Heart)

salt and pepper shakers

What Mulder and Scully wished Donny Pfaster would have collected instead of body parts. (Irresistible)

sample bottles

Generic containers for fat-sucking mutant spit, alien nasal implants, neck implants

belonging to Scully and the gals of MUFON, and antifreeze from the bottom of Darren Oswald's shoe. (2SHY, The X-Files: Pilot, Revelations, D.P.O.)

sand

When found in the lungs of a victim who's several hundred miles from the beach, a fairly strong indication that *something* weird is going on. (Firewalker)

sandbox

A dangerous place to play with toy soldiers when phantom veterans are on the loose. (The Walk)

"sanitized"

Condition of a UFO crash site after one has swept any evidence into bags, bottles, and a variety of containers sporting radiation warning tags, all destined for secret labs and Pentagon basements; after one has "suggested" that eyewitnesses fade into the background; and after one has planted the notion that less cooperative

witnesses might be short a few marbles. (Fallen Angel)

satellite dish

Good place to catch alien autopsy videos at two o'clock in the morning. (Nisei)

sawed-off shotgun

The unusual office equipment mounted on a swivel bracket under Jerry Kallenchuk's desk. (Piper Maru)

screaming monkeys

The X-Filean version of background music. (The Erlenmeyer Flask)

"Skeptics like you make me sick!"

Yappi's scathing denunciation of Mulder. (Clyde Bruckman's Final Repose)

schizophrenia

Scully's excuse for all mental conditions that can't be attributed to her favorite illness, post-traumatic stress syndrome. (Lazarus, etc.)

science

Scully's altar.

screenplay format

How not to organize your UFO abduction report if you want to be taken seriously. (Jose Chung's "From Outer Space")

scruffy minds

Like Brad Wilczek, those likely to enjoy puzzles and conundrums, but find murder a tad repulsive. (Ghost in the Machine)

Special Agent Dana Scully

For a woman who joined the FBI with plans to "distinguish" herself, assignment to the basement offices of the X-Files, and to a partner generally regarded as a bit of a nut, probably wasn't high on her list of priorities.

Since then, however, and in spite of Mulder's tendency to patronize her, she's been an active member of a difficult partnership. While she'll never abandon her insistence on working from a sound scientific premise, Scully's no straitlaced, closed-minded devotee of the "book." In fact, quite the contrary . . .

While still a student at Quantico, and surrounded by the Old Boys' Club, she was secure enough with herself to engage in an open relationship with an instructor—despite the comments such actions might raise.

When even Mulder scoffed at some of the cases she brought in, like the "rape" of a convalescent home nurse, she pursued them with the same tenacity he would have shown.

In some ways, she may even be more open to extreme possibility than her partner—she's not so quick to assume that God, or miracles, can be written off as no more than folklore.

Special Agent Dana Scully, even without Mulder's greater experience, is a force to be reckoned with.

sea legs
Lacking them, Mulder spent most of a twelve-hour trip through Norwegian waters in the head. (Død Kalm)

"secret password"
What you need to be reincarnated. (The List)

secrets
The only real currency the Intelligence Committee deals in. (Nisei)

self-impalement
Dr. Blockhead's vision of appropriate mid-funerary entertainment. (Humbug)

sex
Clyde Bruckman couldn't get any. (Clyde Bruckman's Final Repose)

"set of wheels"
How a hog-rider described Scully. (Conduit)

shadow
Unlike Peter Pan, Dr. Banton would have given almost anything to lose his. (Soft Light)

shadow government
The ultimate in cliches, and, perhaps, the ultimate employer of characters like X and the Cigarette-Smoking Man. If so, Krycek probably doesn't think too much of their retirement package. (Apocrypha)

"signs from God"
Not the strangest things Scully has seen. (Apocrypha)

silo
Unusual garage for an unusual form of transport. (Apocrypha)

sixteenth-century Italian poetry
What you don't want to hear being whispered by your date. (Clyde Bruckman's Final Repose)

skating

Not a skill shared equally by all members of the Lone Gunmen. (Apocrypha)

Walter Sergei Skinner

An assistant director of the FBI, Skinner finds himself in the uncomfortable position of guiding and protecting a pair of agents who seem hell-bent on following their own course—regardless of the consequences.

Though his actions often seem callous and contradictory to Mulder and Scully, a strong moral streak seems to run through everything he does. Whatever his personal beliefs, he won't sacrifice the system, cut judicial corners, or condone actions that clearly violate his own sense of honor—something that has apparently gotten him into hot water with at least one of the power players. If he has, from time to time, slipped Mulder addresses or information, stepped beyond the bounds of his office, or covered their backs, it seems likely that he was more willing to sacrifice Skinner the man than the office he filled.

The demanding nature of his position apparently strained the seams of his personal life as well, to the point where he and wife, Sharon, were on the verge of divorcing.

sleep

What Augustus Cole couldn't get, Mulder didn't want, and Skinner was afraid of. (Sleepless, 3, Avatar)

smallpox vaccine

In most places, a medical miracle; in the X-Files universe, an opportunity to create DNA records of every school-age child. (Paper Clip)

Jeremiah Smith

Owner of one great set of hands. (Talitha Cumi)

Ray Soames

The only person known to have "appeared" in *two* X-Filean graveyards, one on each coast. Not bad air miles for a corpse. (The X-Files: Pilot, Irresistible)

soft light

The most flattering illumination for people like Dr. Banton, who made a living playing with atomic particles the rest of us can't remember the names of. (Soft Light)

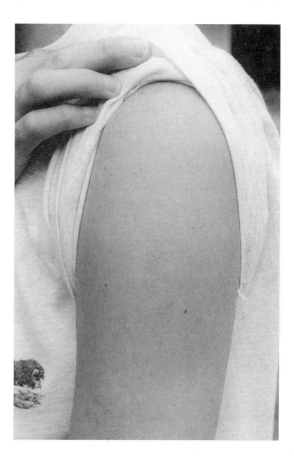

soft water

Not necessarily a first choice for drinking water if you live in Mulder's building. (Anasazi)

solution

Though the Cigarette-Smoking Man claims there's one for every problem, he doesn't seem to have found the solution for a pair of nosy agents. (Sleepless)

"son of a bitch!"

Term of endearment used by all major X-Files characters. (Anasazi, The Blessing Way, Paper Clip)

South Dakota

In addition to being home to hundreds of not-so-empty nuclear silos, it's where Max Fenig suffered his first "epileptic seizure." (Apocrypha, Fallen Angel)

spitting on victims

Stupid thing to do unless you're actually trying to leave evidence at the scene of a crime. (Apocrypha)

spooky

1—More than slightly derogatory nickname pinned on Fox Mulder during his academy days. 2—Scully's description of Lucy Householder's ability to mimic the speech of Amy Jacobs. (Oubliette)

spontaneous human combustion

Though clearly one of Mulder's more cherished theories, not one that's actually panned out for him yet. Instead, he's found one pyrokinetic with a taste for other men's wives and a scientist with a habit of getting too close to his experiments. (Fire, Soft Light)

sports section

Mulder's answer to flight-induced difficulties in producing a stool sample on demand. (Ice)

squeamish

Even Mulder isn't too anxious to wander through sewers, get covered in bile, handle toilet-drowned rats, or touch adipose-reducing goo. (The Host, Tooms, Teso dos Bichos, 2SHY)

"squirrelly"

Mulder description of yage-sipping Dr. Bilac. (Teso dos Bichos)

"Stairway to Heaven"

Mulder's least favorite tune. (Ascension)

statistical aberration

The "official" explanation for the fact that Kevin Morris, a child, was able to reconstruct da Vinci's *Universal Man*, portions of Shakespeare's sonnets, and sections of the Brandenburg Concerto in *binary*. (Conduit)

Stratego

Mulder's been waiting twenty-two years to finish one particular game. (Colony)

street lights

1—Mulder's mother likes him to be home before they come on. (The Erlenmeyer Flask) **2**—Mulder shot two of them. (Soft Light)

stereotypy

Yet another "scientific" explanation offered by Dr. Scully when presented with the oddities of human nature, in this case a man who has made so many fishing flies out of his own hair that he makes Kojak look like one of the Beatles. (Deep Throat)

Strughold Mining Corporation
When coal stopped coming out of a Virginia mountain, a secret consortium started putting something much more valuable inside it. (Paper Clip)

"stick-with-it-ness"
The quality that took the Arctic Ice Core Projects to new depths—and ice worms to new heights where they found scientists and dogs to be equally good hosts. (Ice)

"stylin' " shirts
One of Mulder's many fashion faux pas. (Roland)

subtitles
Frequent feature of an *X-Files* episode. To date, German, Japanese, Italian, Russian, French, Navajo, and Cantonese have been featured.

"Sucker!"
1—How Scully describes an agent who'd pay $20 to a diner waitress for a blurry photo of a "UFO." (Deep Throat) **2**—How Mulder describes an agent who expects to find secret UFO-research facility on a U.S. Geological Survey map. (Deep Throat)

sunflower seeds
Along with a little water, the sum total of all takeout orders Mulder placed while recovering on the Navajo reservation. (The Blessing Way)

"suspicion of homicide by emission of direct electric current"
The charge Mulder and Scully planned to bring against Darren Morgan. (D.P.O.)

swamp gas
Scully's explanation for lights in the skies, Sheriff Arens's explanation for everything from illegal trash burning to foxfire, and Mulder's reaction to Dodger dogs. (The X-Files: Pilot, E.B.E., Our Town)

sweet dreams

What Augustus Cole could have used more of. (Sleepless)

Karen Swenson

Notable as the very first dead body to appear in *The X-Files* (The X-Files: Pilot).

swimming pools

Less than relaxing location for Captain Draper, the Crocodile Man, and Slash victims. For those who jump at an opportunity to see a little more of David Duchovny, locale for the infamous Speedo scene. (The Walk, Humbug, Aubrey, Duane Barry)

swing sets

The final resting place of some unwanted parents. (Eve)

switch-pick

Closely resembling its cousin, the switch-blade, this supposedly alien weapon can be found in the hip pocket of downed UFO pilots or in the lamps of the Mulders' beach house. (End Game, Talitha Cumi)

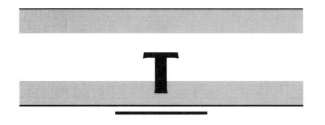

T

target

Scully's role in the capture of John Barnett. She pulled it off beautifully, taking two point-blank shots in her bullet-proofed evening wear.

tasseographer
Tea reader, not a recommended second job for doll collectors in Minnesota. (Clyde Bruckman's Final Repose)

"tasty!"
Frohike's assessment of Mulder's partner. (Blood)

tech-heads
Agent Pendrel's cronies in the Sci-Crime Unit at the FBI. (731)

Ten Commandments
Mulder should take a refresher course in these. (Anasazi)

"terminal force"
Secret agent–speak for the nasty ending awaiting pesky FBI agents with a nose for the bizarre. (Little Green Men)

"Terror of Scotland Yard"
How Mulder describes the only woman we know him to have been intimate with, Phoebe Green. (Fire)

Tetra Meal D
Colonel Buddahas's idea of a condiment. (Deep Throat)

"they"

Depending on circumstances, aliens, other FBI agents, or agents of the NSA, CIA, DND, or other alphabet groups.

things that move by themselves

Door bolts, fire alarm handles, beds, garage doors, federal agents, scarves . . . (The Walk, Excelsius Dei, The Calusari, Born Again, etc.)

Thinker

Fourth member of the Lone Gunmen, he was later known as Kenneth Soona, hacker extraordinaire. (One Breath, Anasazi)

Gerd Thomas

The X-Filean version of the Peeping Tom. (Red Museum)

"three-pipe problem"

What Phoebe Green dangles in front of Mulder to induce him to help her solve a case. (Fire)

Three Stooges

How Mulder describes the Lone Gunmen when *they* come to *him* for help. (Anasazi)

tie-straightening

Obsession of an "NSA" assassin when he's not too busy killing people in bathrooms. (Nisei)

time

Of all four dimensions, the one most likely to be warped in the X-Files universe.

"too much sugar"

Sure way to identify stigmatic hoaxers. (Revelations)

touchpads

They stumped Roland once—and Mulder more often than he'd likely care to remember. (Roland, 731)

traffic lights

Not to be trusted in Darren Peter Oswald's hometown. (D.P.O.)

train conductors

Surprisingly apt students of covert investigation procedures. (Nisei)

tranquilizers

Handy things to have when faced with iceworm-infected dogs or beastwomen. (Ice, The Jersey Devil)

travel agency

Where Duane Barry stopped to get some information on off-planet excursions. (Duane Barry)

trenchcoat

Useful for hiding pregnancies.

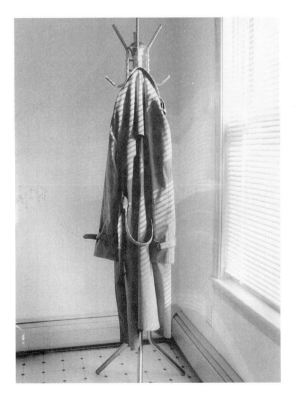

"true American heroes"

Mulder's assessment of the men and women of NASA, his childhood idols, the object of his more mature, if cynical, respect. (Space)

TRUSTNO1

The password that gets you into Mulder's hidden computer records. (Little Green Men)

Truth

An elephant when described piecemeal by three blind men. (Firewalker)

twins

To be automatically filed in the "suspicious characters" section, along with the Eves, Roland and his rocket scientist brother, and little boys who require the attention of Romanian exorcists. (Eve, Roland, The Calusari)

two-parters

Just as department-store Santas herald the coming of Christmas, a two-parter X-File, crammed with aliens and special effects, is a sure sign that it's either sweeps week in Hollyweird or time to frustrate X-Philes for an entire summer.

UFO
Possible explanation for any suspicious event.

"ugly suit"
Mulder's way of identifying CIA agents. (Young at Heart)

"unarmed, but extremely attractive"
How Scully suggests they describe gender-bending Brother Martin. (Gender-Bender)

"Unbelievable!"
Frohike on seeing Mulder alive. Fro' always gets the best lines. (Paper Clip)

underwear

Both Mulder and Scully have shown off their choices for those clothes worn closest to the skin. Both like silk, pink and pretty for Scully, sexy black boxers for Mulder. (The X-Files: Pilot, Fire)

"unknown biological vectors"

Super-secret covert-type speak for glowing green bugs. (Darkness Falls)

"unofficial channels"

Conduit through which all the best information, such as the location of downed alien spacecraft, can be obtained. (End Game)

utility poles

Scully's seen her partner doing some decidedly queer things from time to time, but when he starts climbing utility poles, even she gets worried. (Wetwired)

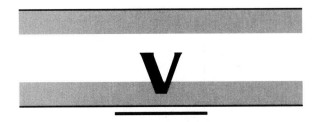

VCS

Violent Crimes Section, Mulder's assignment before taking on the X-Files and moving to the basement.

vampires

One of the few things Mulder claimed *not* to believe in—until his suspect went up in smoke. (3)

van, unmarked

What you don't want to encounter on a bridge, find parked across the road from your house, or have following you at night. Not to mention an incredibly bad vehicle to find yourself trussed in the back of. (The Erlenmeyer Flask)

Vandals

Darren Peter Oswald's favorite band. (D.P.O.)

ventilation fan

Holds the distinction of being one of the few things—other than Mulder—that Scully has actually shot and hit. (Ghost in the Machine)

Venus

As good an explanation as any for "bright-lights in the sky." (Jose Chung's "From Outer Space")

"a very disgruntled altar boy"

One of the many suspects Mulder is willing to consider in "Revelations." Oddly enough, Scully's stigmatic theory, as paranormal as anything Mulder himself could have come up with, gets pooh-poohed by her suddenly cynical partner.

vibuti

The legendary something for nothing. An apport that appeared out of thin air, failed to show up as either organic or inorganic under analysis, and was better known as Holy Ash. Scully didn't buy that or the loaves and fishes story, either. (The Calusari)

video collection

Key item in Mulder's last will and testament. (Paper Clip)

"video piracy thing"

Pseudo-legitimate reason for two federal agents to claim travel expenses, hotel accommodation, and a per-diem on meals while actually tracking down an alien autopsy video even "hokier" than the one shown on the Fox network. (Nisei)

Virtua Fighter 2

A hazardous place to lay a quarter if Darren Peter Oswald wants to play. (D.P.O.)

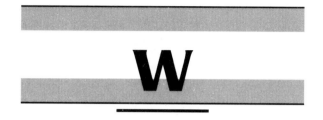

wallpaper
Scully didn't approve of Mulder's new stuff. (Grotesque)

Warden
In the X-Files universe, instantly identifiable as one of the Bad Guys. (The List)

Carl Wade
Part-time photographer with a decidedly perverse choice of subjects. (Oubliette)

Watergate Hotel
Appropriate meeting spot for disenchanted agents. (Little Green Men)

"We just knew"
Less-than-comforting explanation given by the young Eves for the precision timing they managed to achieve while killing their fathers. (Eve)

wedding bands

What Assistant Director Skinner kept hidden away in his desk drawer for three seasons, and what Warren James Dupree came back from the dead to recover. (Talitha Cumi, Lazarus)

Well-Groomed Man

Individual known for his predilection for attending funerals and "predicting" the future by the simple expedient of forcing events into the path determined by him and his consortium. (The Blessing Way)

well-preserved

Almost everyone who lives in Dudley, Arkansas, the home of Chaco Chicken. (Our Town)

"weirder than ours"

How the Lone Gunmen describe Mulder's theories. (E.B.E.)

"weirdness"

Frohike's assessment of the situation after a woman, for no apparent reason, shoots her husband in Mulder's building. Then again, maybe it was the police response time he was discussing. Since when do two cops arrive at any crime scene in less time than it takes one federal agent and three paranoid geniuses to jog down a hallway? (Anasazi)

Dr. Heitz Werber

One of the few people Mulder has allowed to play with his head, Dr. Werber regressed Mulder to the night of Samantha's disappearance and one version of the Truth Mulder is seeking. Dr. Werber's efforts for Billy Miles, however, put Mulder firmly outside the status quo ranks of his colleagues at the FBI. (The X-Files: Pilot)

The Whammy

The scientifically unexplainable, but instinctively recognizable *something* that makes perfect sense at the time, but couldn't stand the scrutiny of even a kangaroo court. (Pusher)

wheelchairs

Convenient places to hide the legs of actors. (The Walk)

white buffalo calves

Better at handing out prognoses than a hospital full of Washington doctors. (Paper Clip)

"wiggy"

Scully's not-so-medical description of men who crawl, screaming, under chairs while watching the news channel. (Wet-wired)

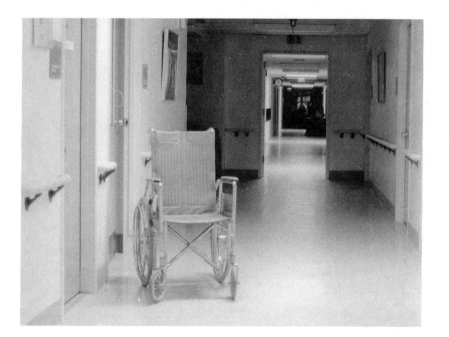

Jack Willis

The man—and FBI Academy instructor—that Scully was willing to date openly while she was still in training, a risky move for a woman with ambitions to "distinguish" herself. His place in her background lends hope to all those fans who wait for "something" to happen between Scully and her partner. (Lazarus)

wiretap duty

Mulder's punishment for indulging in "unofficial" investigations; Scully's seems to have been banishment to the autopsy bays of the Quantico facility. (Little Green Men)

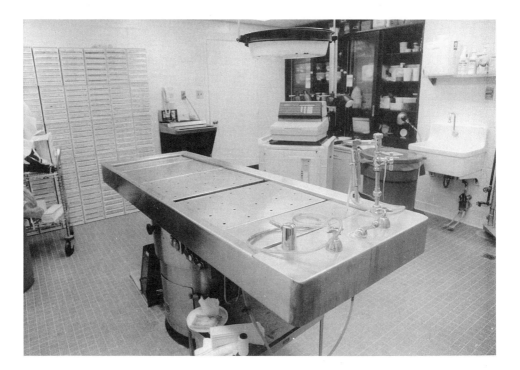

wood-chipper

An unusual, but highly effective, means of suicide. (The Walk)

woods

Place to find cabins with deep basements, hungry women, and little green bugs. Also primary target for teens running about in the night in their pajamas. (Oubliette, The Jersey Devil, Darkness Falls, The X-Files: Pilot)

woody wagons

If the MIBs are famous for their black sedans and black helicopters, it's only fitting that the Good Guys should have some distinctive transport of their own, and what could be *less* threatening than the wood-paneled station wagon favored by such Nicies as Max Fenig and the Traveling Calusari Show? (Fallen Angel, The Calusari)

worldviews

Not satisfied with his own bizarre take on the world, Mulder seems to derive great delight in overturning Scully's more prosaic take on the world. (E.B.E.)

WWII

A thorough knowledge of this topic would help any X-Phile follow the action.

"wouldn't want to date her"

The refrain you don't want to hear issuing from the bleachers of Grover Cleveland Alexander High School. (Syzygy)

wrist restraints

Essential decor element at the Excelsius Dei Convalescent Home. (Excelsius Dei)

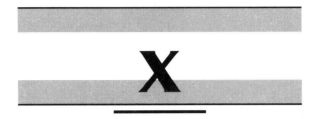

X

X

The mysterious second source that appeared after the premature demise of Deep Throat. Without doubt a double, and possibly triple, agent, X finished the third season by trying to kill Mulder (the same man he saved from a bomb just weeks before), successfully assassinating two of his cohorts, and lying to the Cigarette-Smoking Man. (Wetwired)

X-ray film

What the smart (if spooky) agent will always have on hand to pick up "psychic fingerprints" in case a perpetrator doesn't leave any useful physical evidence.

yage
Probably not a good choice to bring to a pot luck. (Teso dos Bichos)

yahoos
In Mulder's parlance, this group wouldn't include molecular biologists, astrophysicists, or alternative fuel researchers. (War of the Coprophages)

the Stupendous Yappi
Psychic who predicted, among other things, that Madonna would become embroiled in an affair with "super-witness" Kato Kaelin. He failed, however, to provide useful clues to Mulder, whom he described as an unbeliever with "negative energy." (Clyde Bruckman's Final Repose)

"You never draw my bath"
The comment that introduced Mulder's Pouty Look to TV audiences. (Revelations)

Z

Z-14 filter

What an FBI technician used to remove Lula Phillips's nasal tones from an audiotape and reveal background noises so specific that the tech could determine the type, size, altitude, and landing direction of a small plane. Seems a pity they didn't put this technician on that pesky "untraceable" cellular phone problem . . . (Lazarus)

Madam Zelma

Palmist who lacked Mr. Bruckman's ability to foresee her own death, otherwise she'd have closed her shop early on the 16th of September. (Clyde Bruckman's Final Repose)

Zero

Voted "Most Likely to Stick Scissors Into Sockets." (D.P.O.)

Zeus Faber

Found written on the bow of a World War II submarine and along the sides of the yellow pencils crowding most writers' pencil mugs. (Piper Maru)

Madam Zirinka

Unlike Madam Zelma, Zirinka demands ID and a credit check *before* handing out any of her hard-won information. (Syzygy)

Steve Zinnzser

Man whose predilection for pirating videotapes earned him a pillowcase and a bullet. (Nisei)

zipper

Dead giveaway that your "dead alien" was never a live alien. (Jose Chung's "From Outer Space")

Zuni

If Mulder had been tracking down Zuni instead of Anasazi, he'd have had at least a ghost of a chance of reaching those Ancient Aliens. (Anasazi, The Blessing Way)

X | SEASON ONE | X

101
THE X-FILES: PILOT

With sunflower seeds and skepticism packed for the trip, Mulder and Scully head out for small-town Oregon to investigate the deaths of three teenagers who, after graduating in the same class, went on to spend the next several years sharing a psychiatric ward.

CATCH IT!

With at least three years of seeing her in power suits and trenchcoats, fans of Gillian Anderson will have to make do with their brief glimpse of her in something more revealing in "The X-Files: Pilot"

102
DEEP THROAT

When a missing test pilot's wife calls in the FBI, Scully and Mulder find themselves on the wrong side of a high-security fence. Getting inside, however, only raises more questions—questions that Mulder's new and mysterious source seems reluctant to resolve.

103
SQUEEZE

With a knack for squeezing down chimneys and up drain pipes, serial killer Eugene Victor Tooms proves equally adept at squirming out of custody. With the FBI pressing for conventional evidence and time ticking away, Mulder and Scully find themselves in a tight professional corner as the body count mounts.

104
CONDUIT

When a former abductee's daughter disappears from the same location, no one seems ready to listen—no one except Mulder. His job is made even more difficult by Scully's staunch belief that this investigation is less about Ruby Morris than it is about Samantha Scully.

105
THE JERSEY DEVIL

Mulder's trip to Atlantic City doesn't take him to the glittering casinos or luxury hotels. Instead, he plays a dangerous game of hunter-and-hunted with the maneater that haunts the back alleys of and woods surrounding the city. However, it's not long before even Scully, the eternal skeptic, is lured back by the mounting evidence Mulder manages to drag out of tourist-wary local law enforcement agencies.

CATCH IT!

"The Jersey Devil" is notable for its value in determining Mulder's taste in women.

106
SHADOWS

Disparate incidents begin to come together after Scully and Mulder dig up a bizarre photo taken during an ATM robbery. Hovering in the background, behind a young woman remarkable only for her position with a Defense Department contractor, a ghostly figure leads the agents toward his murderers.

107
GHOST IN THE MACHINE

A new intelligence gropes its way to life in the depths of wires and circuit boards—only to find itself perched on the edge of immediate extinction. When it fights back, killing Mulder's former partner in the process, he and Scully must find a way past its considerable defenses.

108
ICE

At the height of their mutual success, members of a group of scientists start killing one another off. Mulder and Scully, arriving in the far north, discover a life form that survives at the cost of human life. Under the intense pressure of a self-imposed quarantine, Mulder and Scully's fledgling trust is sorely tested.

109
SPACE

A communications specialist from NASA brings evidence of sabotage in the space program, and Mulder's youthful hero-worship is shaken by the apparent involvement of a high-ranking astronaut.

110
FALLEN ANGEL

When a tract of lonely woodland is cordoned off between laser fences, and rapidly changing explanations are rampant, Mulder's curiosity carries him beyond the bounds of official jurisdiction—and into the middle of a UFO cleanup. Scully's attempts to protect Mulder from himself are only marginally successful, and neither agent seems capable of protecting the one innocent on the scene—Max Fenig.

CATCH IT !

In "Fallen Angel," Scully finally gets to work on **live** *patients!*

111
EVE

Two identical girls, two identical deaths, two opposite ends of the country. The connection? An *in vitro* clinic and an even older experiment. As Mulder and Scully attempt to trace the "family tree," it's difficult to separate victims from conspirators.

112
FIRE

When Mulder's old flame arrives in America to chase down an unusual pyromaniac, sparks fly on more than one front. Attempting to overcome a lingering fear of fire, while juggling emotions he'd thought safely buried, proves more difficult than Mulder anticipates. Luckily for him, Scully's more prosaic investigation turns up the clues that allow him to finally douse several fires.

CATCH IT!

Along with a touch of the green-eyed monster, viewers get a glimpse of Mulder's black boxers in this "Fire."

113
BEYOND THE SEA

Returning to work immediately after her father's unexpected death, Scully finds herself frighteningly vulnerable to the charismatic Luther Lee Boggs, who promises her just one more chance to touch her father's soul. All she has to do is support his bid to avoid the death chamber for a series of brutal murders.

114
GENDERBENDER

When a serial killer of indeterminate sex leaves a trail of male and female victims behind, Mulder and Scully must seek a motive and hope it leads to an identity. The motive, however, leads to an entire community and a lifestyle more bizarre than either partner could have conceived.

CATCH IT !

Scully's had two "dates" since joining the X-Files division—bet she wants to forget the one in "GenderBender."

116
YOUNG AT HEART

A new case stirs up painful memories for Mulder when a modern murderer resurrects the M.O. of John Barnett, who had the nasty habit of killing off Mulder's associates. Mulder's growing suspicion that this isn't a copycat, but the dead Barnett himself, doesn't go over well at all.

115
LAZARUS

During a stakeout gone bad, Scully's former lover, Agent Jack Willis, is shot down along with murderer Warren Dupree. As Dupree dies on a nearby gurney, Scully's stubborn efforts appear to save Willis from a similar fate. Mulder, however, isn't so sure . . . Unburdened by any emotional baggage, he's less willing to put aside the psychological and physical discrepancies creeping into Willis's personality.

CATCH IT !

*For all those waiting for a touch of **Who's the Boss?** to invade **The X-Files**, "Young at Heart" nixed the notion that Scully doesn't date other agents.*

117
E.B.E.

A dramatic increase in UFO sightings and a bizarre attack on a transport truck convince Mulder that he's on the trail of a live alien being covertly transported cross-country. For her part, Scully, equally wary of the involvement of the Lone Gunmen as she is of Deep Throat, suspects a rather more earthly explanation.

118
MIRACLE MAN

A rash of deaths under the Miracle Ministry's traveling tent brings Scully and Mulder into the realm of miracles and shysters. When Samuel, reputed raiser of the dead and healer of the sick, indicates he has some knowledge of Mulder's long-lost sister, Scully's convinced the young man is setting them up. Mulder isn't so sure.

119
SHAPES

When a rancher claims to have shot a wild animal, but ends up with a dead Indian youth on his property, Mulder searches for evidence of lycanthropy. Scully, unconvinced by elongated teeth, shed skin, and animal tracks that become human, suggests they dig a little deeper in the land claims history between the touchy neighbors.

120
DARKNESS FALLS

The woods of Washington State are swallowing people without a trace. Suspecting that the disappearances directly relate to the ongoing argument between a logging company and local environmentalists, Scully is ready to ignore reports of little green bugs that can lift a man into the trees—until she finds a man-sized cocoon dangling forty feet above the ground.

121
TOOMS

A psychiatric review board, in all its wisdom, has decided that Eugene Victor Tooms is no longer a threat to himself or society. Mulder and Scully know better. Defying the "book" and its confining regulations, they risk censure and worse to dig even deeper into the earlier murders.

CATCH IT !

To maintain the artistic integrity of the scene beneath the escalator in "Tooms," Doug Hutchison performed it nude except for some yellow goo that, unfortunately, had a habit of sticking to the floor as he crawled . . .

122
BORN AGAIN

When Michelle Bishop is present at two murders in as many days, and the two victims turn out to have a common past, Mulder begins to suspect that the eight-year-old is more than an idle observer. His eventual claim that the child is, somehow, the reincarnation of yet another dead cop threatens to alienate the girl's mother as well as his partner.

123
ROLAND

One by one, the members of a jet propulsion team are being killed. Mysterious notations left at the scene would seem to eliminate the only suspect, a mentally challenged janitor, but Mulder's not so sure and is determined to discover the link.

124
THE ERLENMEYER FLASK

Deep Throat's subtle hints lead Mulder and Scully to a secret project that includes alien DNA in its "gene therapy," but as they race to collect evidence, their witnesses begin dying under distinctly unnatural circumstances.

201
LITTLE GREEN MEN

The X-Files are wrapped in plastic. With Scully safely tucked away at Quantico, and Mulder nearly buried under ordinary wiretap operations, it seems their superiors are determined to keep the former partners from collaborating on any additional cases. That scheme falls apart, however, when, independently, they make their way to a remote area of Puerto Rico where mysterious signals are disturbing the night.

202
THE HOST

Fully expecting to have every time-wasting case the Bureau can come up with dumped in his lap, Mulder is ready to brush off the next assignment Skinner hands him—until Scully finds a bizarre parasite lurking in the latest cadaver's body. Intrigued, the pair begin to piece together a complex chain of events that may lead back to radiation-blasted Chernobyl.

CATCH IT !

"The Host" features one of the best put-together-from-various-animals impersonations of a human chest cavity on TV!

203
BLOOD

Acting out uncontrollable fears, otherwise normal citizens of smalltown America are suddenly turning into mass murderers. The connection proves elusive, even after Mulder and Scully discover that small-town America is the testing site for a deadly new form of "pest control."

204
SLEEPLESS

The last remaining members of an incredibly successful deep-penetration squad are being methodically killed. The surgically altered soldiers have plenty of time to look over their shoulders; they haven't slept since the Vietnam War. Unfortunately, no one seems interested in remembering them, much less protecting them—especially from one another.

205
DUANE BARRY

When an ex-FBI agent who claims to be an abductee escapes from a psychiatric hospital, taking four hostages in the process, Mulder is quickly called in. The hostage team, however, isn't so sure they've made the right call when Mulder begins to buy into Duane Barry's fantasy. Neither is Scully when she discovers *why* Duane Barry was so carefully confined.

206
ASCENSION

Scully's been kidnapped and Mulder is being told, none too politely, to stay out of it. Some chance. Having long since lost faith in his superiors, Mulder begins his own methodical investigation, an investigation that would lead him back to Duane Barry, but not to his partner—not yet.

207
3

Truly alone for the first time since Scully found her way to the basement of the J. Edgar Hoover Building, Mulder throws himself into his work, and into the bizarre world of the vampire-fetishist in search of a trio of serial killers.

CATCH IT!

Thought "3" sizzled? It should have, with Perrey Reeves, then the real-life squeeze of David Duchovny, on screen.

208
ONE BREATH

Appearing out of nowhere, poisoned by a mutated version of her own DNA, Dana Scully hovers on the brink of death. Her abductors have already disappeared. Her family stands ready to honor her Living Will if it should come to that. Mulder's frustration could easily have led him into senseless violence, if not for the unexpected arrival of Melissa Scully.

209
FIREWALKER

Communications with the human members of the Firewalker volcanic research team have failed, but images from the on-site robot include a brief glimpse of a dead body and the shadow of something moving *inside* the volcano. It appears that Scully's first case since her return may be one of the most demanding of her career.

CATCH IT!

"Firewalker" is just one more illustration of why you gotta love X-Filean science!

210
RED MUSEUM

When Wisconsin teens begin staggering, half-naked, from the woods with mysterious messages scrawled over their backs, Mulder and Scully are hard put to find a single suspect. A vegetarian sect, a pedophile Peeping Tom, and one of their own old enemies are so tightly entangled that it may be impossible to identify the culprits before the evidence disappears.

211
EXCELSIUS DEI

When Scully opens a case of her own, the "entity rape" of a nurse in a convalescent home, Mulder's less supportive than she might have expected. Despite his skepticism, she presses the investigation, and he's startled to discover just how accurate his partner's intuitions prove to be.

212
AUBREY

A small-town cop turns up the bones of not one but *two* FBI agents missing for nearly fifty years—but can't explain how she did it. Suspecting some connection between the agents' deaths and a series of modern crimes, Mulder and Scully prepare to separate dreams from reality, memories, and history, and the present from the past—something this young policewoman seems completely unable to do on her own.

213
IRRESISTIBLE

Called in to profile—and catch—a fetishist with an irresistible and growing hankering for lady's fingers, Scully is disturbed on a primal level. When the killer's fixation turns to Scully, and she disappears from a car run off the road, Mulder's clinical detachment is severely shaken.

CATCH IT !

"Irresistible" offers proof that, with a little morphing, **any** *good cop show can be* **The X-Files.**

214
DIE HAND DIE VERLETZT

Claims of ritual killings bring Scully and Mulder to a town where frogs fall from the sky and water runs backwards. As they attempt to investigate the deaths of two teens, locals increase their whispers of woodland altars and dark masses, interfering with Scully's investigation of a substitute teacher no one remembers hiring and Mulder's tracking of an old-country religion.

215
FRESH BONES

Investigating the apparent suicides of two Marines at a camp for Haitian nationals, Mulder and Scully are confronted with claims and counterclaims of authorized beatings, ritual curses, and grave-robbing. Determining what is fact and what is fiction becomes increasingly difficult as the two agents are surrounded by Haiti's magic.

216
COLONY

Identical doctors in identical jobs are being killed all up and down the eastern seaboard. When their obituaries find their way into Mulder's e-mail box, he starts out to investigate their deaths, only to be confronted by a woman claiming to be Samantha Mulder.

217
END GAME

With his sister designated as the only acceptable ransom for his kidnapped partner, Mulder calls in his markers and lays a frantic plan to retain both women. It all goes horribly wrong in the center of a remote bridge, and Samantha is lost. When the trail leads him to Alaska and into the grip of some alien disease, it's up to Scully to determine what, if anything, can save his life.

218
FEARFUL SYMMETRY

Invisible animals are rampaging through town, destroying property and trampling a federal employee. On arriving in town, the agents begin their search at a nearby zoo with the distinction of *never* being the site of a live birth. Whether that's because, as Mulder suspects, aliens are "harvesting" the young or, as Scully insists, an animal rights group is determined to close

down the zoo, the only reliable witness appears to be a hand-signing gorilla named Sophie.

219
DØD KALM

The USS *Ardent* has disappeared inside an area Mulder might dub the northern Bermuda Triangle, and Mulder's determined to find it. The real mystery, however, doesn't come to light until the agents find themselves stranded on a ghost ship that's aging almost as fast as the remains of its crew.

CATCH IT!

With the addition of Norwegian in "Død Kalm," The X-Files *becomes the most subtitled program ever to air in English-speaking markets.*

220
HUMBUG

When a community of circus and side-show performers is terrorized by the mythical Fegee Mermaid, which walks on fins and burrows into its victims, it's up to Mulder and Scully to separate truth from "humbug." Surrounded by tattooed men, bearded ladies, and people who like to retract their testicles, it's probably impossible to come up with an "average" suspect, but even they are shocked when the killer is revealed.

221
THE CALUSARI

A balloon traveling into the face of the wind isn't much of a clue to launch an investigation into a toddler's death, but, on their arrival, a series of bizarre events convinces Scully they're dealing with a rare form of child abuse. For his part, Mulder thinks answers may be found with a pair of dead roosters and a group of elderly chanters called the Calusari.

222
F. EMASCULATA

Mulder and Scully are ordered to assist the federal marshal's office in its search for two inmates who've concealed themselves in the laundry and escaped from a prison. There's no mention, however, of the highly contagious and deadly disease that, coincidentally, broke out just days before the escape. Whether it's an outright attempt to simply eliminate the agents, or an effort to discredit them, remains to be seen.

223
SOFT LIGHT

When people start disappearing, and the case is shoved in her general direction, Detective Kelly Ryan, one of Scully's former students, turns to her old teacher for assistance. Mulder's theories, in fact his very presence, become more and more *un*welcome as the body count continues to mount in his general vicinity. Mulder's growing disinclination to share his thoughts on the case in the face of Ryan's—and Scully's!—evident skepticism doesn't endear him to the women, either.

224
OUR TOWN

When a federal employee suddenly disappears in the Chicken Capital of Arkansas, and his rare, noncontagious disease crops up in a statistically impossible number of his neighbors, Scully begins to wonder if he hasn't been turned into chicken feed. The discovery of dozens of oddly mutilated skeletons, however, has Mulder on a different trail that leads to the chicken plant *owner's* odd eating habits.

225
ANASAZI

Mulder's drawn deeper than ever before into a dangerous world of conspiracies— and his career, his family, his very life could be at stake. Trying to find answers, both partners are in for a shock when Scully takes him to the one man who can decode sensitive documents recording the government's involvement in alien contact.

X SEASON THREE X

301
THE BLESSING WAY

It seems that reports of Mulder's death have been "greatly exaggerated" when he survives the bombing of the boxcar to continue his investigation of clues provided by the Thinker. Cut off from official support once again, both partners turn to unexpected sources for information and support.

CATCH IT !

If the back of a gunshot wound is always bigger than the front, "The Blessing Way" leaves you wondering if Scully didn't shoot her partner in the back! Ooops!

302
PAPER CLIP

When Mulder, more determined than ever to get to the bottom of his personal mystery, and Scully, pursuing her sister's shooter, can once again join forces, their efforts lead them to a mountain vault. There they discover that they have even more reason to trust no one but each other—and that the conspiracy they've stumbled on will require all the resources they can marshal.

303
D.P.O.

When a small town chalks up five lightning-related deaths, Mulder suspects something is amiss in rural America. Despite the apparent validity of the autopsy results Mulder asks her to review, Scully, for once, finds herself in perfect agreement with her partner—especially when the suspect jump-starts his boss's heart—bare-handed.

304
CLYDE BRUCKMAN'S FINAL REPOSE

While investigating a serial killer with a thing for fortune-tellers, Scully and Mulder encounter Clyde Bruckman, who *knows* things that no one outside the crime scene team should know. Scully is ready to place him firmly in the "suspect" category; Mulder, however, suspects he may finally have found proof that clairvoyance—and even predestination—exist.

305
THE LIST

Neetch Manley had plans for his afterlife, a to-do list if you like. He still had five men to kill. Prison officials were ready to simply wipe their hands of their "prison philosopher" and his rantings. The growing pile of bodies, however, was making that rather difficult when Mulder and Scully arrived.

CATCH IT!

*Of all the episodes to date, "The List" is the only one to feature **both** Scully and Mulder powerless to do anything to stop the crimes.*

306
2 SHY

A serial killer with unusual tastes is doing his stalking on the Internet, luring women to him by capitalizing on their vulnerabilities, using his knack for playing into their most desperate desires. His "long distance" approach makes apprehension difficult—and complicating Scully and Mulder's investigations further is his habit of digesting his dates, making it nearly impossible to identify his victims.

307
THE WALK

One soldier has already killed himself, and another is desperately trying to duplicate that feat when Mulder arrives, already convinced that a "phantom soldier" is at work. Scully's more traditional theories quickly lead them to the killer's accomplice, but seem to have failed when the supposed killer himself turns out to be a quadruple amputee.

308
OUBLIETTE

When Mulder's more esoteric notions and Scully's forensic evidence conflict, he finds himself at odds not only with his partner and local law enforcement, but with the woman he's trying to defend! If he stands any chance of recovering the latest young woman in a line of kidnappings, he'll have to teach his partner to believe in the unquantifiable, and a previous victim to believe in herself.

309
NISEI

Mulder's near-playful investigation of his $29.95 alleged alien autopsy video takes a deadly turn when the video's producer is murdered and an old Japanese plot is implicated. In the process of contacting the man's known friends, Scully meets members of the local branch of MUFON. She is shocked to discover a group of female abductees among the membership, a group of women who all know her!

310
731

Ignoring Scully's warnings, Mulder hitches a ride aboard a train carrying an unusual passenger in its quarantine car—only to discover he's walked into a trap. Scully, picking up the threads of the investigation, quickly realizes her involvement stretches back to her own abduction—and beyond. Somewhere in that past she has to find the key to open Mulder's prison.

311
REVELATIONS

Mulder's busy playing skeptic in a case featuring a serial killer and a string of supposed stigmatics when Scully starts noticing things that just don't fit Mulder's worldview. The scent of flowers, an incorruptible corpse, words of prophecy, and her own growing belief in a young man bearing the marks of crucifixion add up to a modern-day miracle for her, but it's a belief she's ill-equipped to defend after a lifetime of reliance on science.

312
WAR OF THE COPROPHAGES

Escaping from his apartment, which is being fumigated, Mulder heads for Martha's Vineyard, where a series of glowing lights have been seen in the sky. Scully, who has certainly earned a few hours' downtime, finds herself becoming intrigued with the bizarre events Mulder encounters, eventually abandoning her ice cream–munching and puppy-washing weekend to join him in a town convinced it's been invaded by killer cockroaches.

CATCH IT !

So? You wanted to know how Scully and Mulder spend their free time? "War of the Coprophages" shows it's not so different from how they spend their workdays!

313
SYZYGY

Instead of horned beasts, pentagrams, and midnight masses—the stuff of which a Satanic cult investigation should be made—Mulder and Scully are confounded by a haunting perfume, malfunctioning TVs, killer garage springs, and two teenage girls best described as . . . cosmic.

314
GROTESQUE

When Special Agent William Patterson, stern hero of the Behavioral Sciences Unit, asks to have his wayward former student assigned to a disturbing case, Mulder is less than thrilled. As the tension mounts between the two implacable egos and theories come into conflict, Scully's own suspicions that Patterson is working to a hidden agenda take shape. Whether Mulder will believe her, or even acknowledge her as he slips deeper into a world of demons and gargoyles, as well as the cesspool of a killer's mind, remains to be seen.

315
PIPER MARU

From the thousands of facts to cross his desk each day, Mulder makes a connection between the mysterious *Talapus,* which he believes carried a downed UFO, and a second ship, the French *Piper Maru,* that recently limped into harbor with a crew dying of radiation exposure. Scully, however, is making links of her own, links that lead her back to her own childhood and her sister's murder.

316
APOCRYPHA

The *Piper Maru*'s place in current events begins to become clear when Scully makes one last connection—between the shooting of A.D. Skinner and that of her sister—while Mulder tracks the path of the elusive wreckage they both believe is responsible for deaths stretching back to 1953. When former agent Alex Krycek turns up once again, it's difficult not to believe the connection will come full circle.

317
PUSHER

The body count rises quickly wherever Pusher goes, but, with dozens of witnesses who swear the deaths were suicides, not murder, Mulder and Scully must track a charismatic killer capable of "convincing" others to do anything he wants. Far from intimidated by the intense interest of a pair of FBI agents, their suspect treats them as new players, pulling them deeper into his intimate—and deadly—game.

318
TESO DOS BICHOS

One scientist dies in Ecuador, another in Boston, a protest letter arrives at the State Department, an unusual artifact leaves its home, and a fervent activist starts acting "squirrelly." Taken together, that adds up to politically motivated murder for Scully, but, not surprisingly, to something considerably more bizarre for Mulder. However, when Scully's suspect disappears from her custody, and from a windowless, doorless room, Mulder's theories begin to seem almost plausible.

319
HELL MONEY

How do you put cuffs on a ghost? That's a question Mulder and Scully may have to answer quickly after arriving in San Francisco's Chinatown to investigate a series of deaths featuring crematory ovens as murder weapons and ancestral spirits as suspects. On finding an astonishing vari-

ety of organs missing from her autopsy subjects, however, Dana Scully begins looking for a more "solid" suspect.

320
JOSE CHUNG'S "FROM OUTER SPACE"

Scully's attempts to re-create the events surrounding an alien abduction for docu-novel writer Jose Chung become complicated as they try to reconcile the statements of a score of eyewitnesses, all operating with their own agendas and prejudices. The truth, she discovers, even for FBI agents, is both elusive and illusionary. Despite being given this second chance to record the "facts," Scully herself has difficulty reconciling the case's primary evidence with the eyewitness testimony.

321
AVATAR

Assistant Director Walter Skinner discovers how quickly the tables can turn when he wakes up with a dead prostitute in his bed, and it's Scully and Mulder who must try to prove his innocence to both the police and the Office of Professional Conduct. Skinner's natural reticence and an incredibly inconvenient bout of amnesia conspire to make their job more difficult, but it's Cigarette-Smoking Man's shadowy presence that may prove the most ominous.

CATCH IT !

If you ever wondered what Skinner looked like **with** *hair, "Avatar" answers that question.*

322
QUAGMIRE

Giving up a well-deserved weekend off to help Mulder investigate a series of missing persons reports seems like a legitimate, if routine, enterprise to Scully—until she discovers his prime suspect is an American version of the Loch Ness Monster! When bits and pieces of tourists and residents beginning bobbing up all over the lake, even Scully is willing to admit something unusual is afoot in and around Heuvelman's Lake.

323
WETWIRED

Scully's involvement in their latest case becomes personal when, after hours spent staring at the evidence, in this case stacks of videotape, she "catches" the same violent paranoia afflicting their suspects—then disappears. With his partner reduced to just one more suspect in a series of violent assaults, Mulder's duties and his loyalties work against each other and the truth may even get lost in the shuffle.

324
TALITHA CUMI

After arriving at what should be one of their bloodiest crime scenes, Mulder and Scully are shocked to discover the gunman's victims miraculously healed and their mysterious benefactor missing from the scene. The hunt for Jeremiah Smith intensifies when Scully discovers a series of identical men, hauntingly similar to the cloned Gregors, stretching across the country.

1992

J	F	M	A	M	J
1 We	1 Sa	1 Su	1 We	1 Fr	1 Mo
2 Th	2 Su	2 Mo	2 Th	2 Sa	2 Tu
3 Fr	3 Mo	3 Tu	3 Fr	3 Su	3 We
4 Sa	4 Tu	4 We	4 Sa	4 Mo	4 Th
5 Su	5 We	5 Th	5 Su	5 Tu	5 Fr
6 Mo	6 Th	6 Fr *Scully - Blevins*	6 Mo	6 We *"N.B." Deep Throat notes to be included on general ledger.*	6 Sa
7 Tu	7 Fr	7 Sa *Scully joins X-Files*	7 Tu	7 Th	7 Su
8 We	8 Sa	8 Su	8 We	8 Fr	8 Mo
9 Th	9 Su	9 Mo *First Case*	9 Th	9 Sa	9 Tu
10 Fr	10 Mo	10 Tu *(Oregon)*	10 Fr	10 Su	10 We
11 Sa	11 Tu	11 We *-4 days of field work*	11 Sa	11 Mo	11 Th
12 Su	12 We	12 Th *-10 days*	12 Su	12 Tu	12 Fr
13 Mo	13 Th	13 Fr *follow up,*	13 Mo	13 We	13 Sa
14 Tu	14 Fr	14 Sa *Wash. Bureau*	14 Tu	14 Th	14 Su
15 We	15 Sa	15 Su	15 We	15 Fr	15 Mo
16 Th	16 Su	16 Mo	16 Th	16 Sa	16 Tu
17 Fr	17 Mo	17 Tu	17 Fr	17 Su	17 We
18 Sa	18 Tu	18 We	18 Sa	18 Mo	18 Th
19 Su	19 We	19 Th	19 Su	19 Tu	19 Fr
20 Mo	20 Th	20 Fr	20 Mo	20 We	20 Sa
21 Tu	21 Fr	21 Sa	21 Tu	21 Th	21 Su
22 We *Samantha's Birthday*	22 Sa *Scully! Jack's Birthday*	22 Su *Billy Miles! FBI HQ*	22 We	22 Fr	22 Mo
23 Th	23 Su	23 Mo	23 Th	23 Sa	23 Tu
24 Fr	24 Mo	24 Tu	24 Fr	24 Su	24 We
25 Sa	25 Tu	25 We	25 Sa	25 Mo	25 Th
26 Su	26 We	26 Th	26 Su	26 Tu	26 Fr
27 Mo	27 Th	27 Fr	27 Mo	27 We	27 Sa
28 Tu	28 Fr	28 Sa	28 Tu	28 Th	28 Su
29 We	29 Sa	29 Su	29 We	29 Fr	29 Mo
30 Th		30 Mo	30 Th	30 Sa	30 Tu
31 Fr		31 Tu		31 Su	

1992

JULY	AUGUST	SEPTEMBER	OCTOBER	NOVEMBER	DECEMBER
1 We	1 Sa	1 Tu	1 Th	1 Su	1 Tu
2 Th	2 Su	2 We	2 Fr	2 Mo	2 We
3 Fr	3 Mo	3 Th	3 Sa	3 Tu	3 Th
4 Sa	4 Tu	4 Fr	4 Su	4 We	4 Fr
5 Su	5 We	5 Sa	5 Mo	5 Th	5 Sa
6 Mo	6 Th	6 Su	6 Tu	6 Fr	6 Su
7 Tu	7 Fr	7 Mo	7 We	7 Sa	7 Mo
8 We	8 Sa	8 Tu	8 Th	8 Su	8 Tu
9 Th	9 Su	9 We	9 Fr	9 Mo	9 We
10 Fr	10 Mo	10 Th	10 Sa	10 Tu	10 Th
11 Sa	11 Tu	11 Fr	11 Su *Mulder's Birthday?*	11 We	11 Fr
12 Su	12 We	12 Sa	12 Mo	12 Th	12 Sa
13 Mo	13 Th	13 Su	13 Tu	13 Fr	13 Su
14 Tu	14 Fr	14 Mo	14 We	14 Sa	14 Mo
15 We	15 Sa	15 Tu	15 Th	15 Su	15 Tu
16 Th	16 Su	16 We *Anniversary Barnett's RIP*	16 Fr	16 Mo	16 We
17 Fr	17 Mo	17 Th	17 Sa	17 Tu	17 Th
18 Sa	18 Tu	18 Fr	18 Su	18 We	18 Fr
19 Su	19 We	19 Sa	19 Mo	19 Th	19 Sa
20 Mo	20 Th	20 Su	20 Tu	20 Fr	20 Su
21 Tu	21 Fr	21 Mo	21 We	21 Sa	21 Mo
22 We	22 Sa	22 Tu	22 Th	22 Su	22 Tu
23 Th	23 Su	23 We	23 Fr	23 Mo	23 We
24 Fr	24 Mo	24 Th	24 Sa	24 Tu	24 Th
25 Sa	25 Tu	25 Fr	25 Su	25 We	25 Fr
26 Su	26 We	26 Sa	26 Mo	26 Th	26 Sa
27 Mo	27 Th	27 Su	27 Tu	27 Fr *Anniversary of Sam's Abduction*	27 Su
28 Tu	28 Fr	28 Mo	28 We	28 Sa	28 Mo
29 We	29 Sa	29 Tu	29 Th	29 Su	29 Tu
30 Th	30 Su	30 We	30 Fr	30 Mo	30 We
31 Fr	31 Mo		31 Sa		31 Th

1993

January	February	March	April	May	June
1 Fr	1 Mo	1 Mo	1 Th	1 Sa	1 Tu
2 Sa	2 Tu	2 Tu	2 Fr	2 Su	2 We
3 Su	3 We	3 We	3 Sa	3 Mo	3 Th
4 Mo	4 Th	4 Th	4 Su	4 Tu	4 Fr
5 Tu	5 Fr	5 Fr	5 Mo	5 We	5 Sa
6 We	6 Sa	6 Sa	6 Tu	6 Th	6 Su
7 Th	7 Su	7 Su	7 We	7 Fr	7 Mo
8 Fr	8 Mo	8 Mo	8 Th	8 Sa	8 Tu
9 Sa	9 Tu	9 Tu	9 Fr	9 Su	9 We
10 Su	10 We	10 We	10 Sa	10 Mo	10 Th
11 Mo	11 Th	11 Th	11 Su	11 Tu	11 Fr
12 Tu	12 Fr	12 Fr	12 Mo	12 We	12 Sa
13 We	13 Sa	13 Sa	13 Tu	13 Th	13 Su
14 Th	14 Su	14 Su	14 We	14 Fr	14 Mo
15 Fr	15 Mo	15 Mo	15 Th	15 Sa	15 Tu
16 Sa	16 Tu	16 Tu	16 Fr	16 Su	16 We
17 Su	17 We	17 We	17 Sa	17 Mo	17 Th
18 Mo	18 Th	18 Th	18 Su	18 Tu	18 Fr
19 Tu	19 Fr	19 Fr	19 Mo	19 We	19 Sa
20 We	20 Sa	20 Sa	20 Tu	20 Th	20 Su
21 Th	21 Su	21 Su	21 We	21 Fr	21 Mo
22 Fr	22 Mo	22 Mo	22 Th	22 Sa	22 Tu
23 Sa	23 Tu	23 Tu	23 Fr	23 Su	23 We
24 Su	24 We	24 We	24 Sa	24 Mo	24 Th
25 Mo	25 Th	25 Th	25 Su	25 Tu	25 Fr
26 Tu	26 Fr	26 Fr	26 Mo	26 We	26 Sa
27 We	27 Sa	27 Sa	27 Tu	27 Th	27 Su
28 Th	28 Su	28 Su	28 We	28 Fr	28 Mo
29 Fr	29 Mo	29 Mo	29 Th	29 Sa	29 Tu
30 Sa		30 Tu	30 Fr	30 Su	30 We
31 Su		31 We		31 Mo	

JULY	AUGUST	SEPTEMBER	OCTOBER	NOVEMBER	DECEMBER
1 We	1 Sa	1 Tu	1 Th	1 Su	1 Tu
2 Th	2 Su	2 We	2 Fr	2 Mo	2 We
3 Fr	3 Mo	3 Th	3 Sa	3 Tu	3 Th
4 Sa	4 Tu	4 Fr	4 Su	4 We	4 Fr
5 Su	5 We	5 Sa	5 Mo *"Shadows" closes*	5 Th	5 Sa
6 Mo	6 Th	6 Su	6 Tu	6 Fr	6 Su *"Eve"*
7 Tu	7 Fr	7 Mo	7 We	7 Sa *"Ice" Quarantine? 3 day Q?*	7 Mo
8 We	8 Sa	8 Tu	8 Th	8 Su	8 Tu
9 Th	9 Su *"The Jersey Devil"*	9 We	9 Fr	9 Mo	9 We
10 Fr	10 Mo	10 Th	10 Sa	10 Tu	10 Th
11 Sa	11 Tu	11 Fr	11 Su	11 We *"Ice" ends*	11 Fr
12 Su	12 We	12 Sa	12 Mo	12 Th	12 Sa
13 Mo	13 Th	13 Su	13 Tu	13 Fr	13 Su *"Fire"*
14 Tu	14 Fr	14 Mo	14 We	14 Sa	14 Mo
15 We	15 Sa	15 Tu	15 Th	15 Su	15 Tu
16 Th	16 Su	16 We	16 Fr	16 Mo *"Space"*	16 We
17 Fr	17 Mo	17 Th	17 Sa	17 Tu	17 Th
18 Sa	18 Tu	18 Fr	18 Su	18 We	18 Fr
19 Su	19 We	19 Sa	19 Mo	19 Th	19 Sa
20 Mo *"Squeeze"*	20 Th	20 Su	20 Tu	20 Fr	20 Su
21 Tu *Notes on in general ledger*	21 Fr	21 Mo	21 We	21 Sa	21 Mo
22 We	22 Sa	22 Tu	22 Th	22 Su *"Fallen Angel"*	22 Tu
23 Th *Tooms in custody*	23 Su	23 We	23 Fr *"Ghost in the Machine"*	23 Tu	23 We
24 Fr	24 Mo	24 Th	24 Sa	24 Tu	24 Th
25 Sa	25 Tu	25 Fr	25 Su	25 We	25 Fr
26 Su	26 We *"Conduit"*	26 Sa *"Shadows" opens*	26 Mo	26 Th	26 Sa
27 Mo	27 Th	27 Su	27 Tu	27 Fr	27 Su
28 Tu	28 Fr	28 Mo	28 We	28 Sa	28 Mo *"Beyond the Sea"*
29 We	29 Sa	29 Tu	29 Th	29 Su	29 Tu
30 Th	30 Su	30 We	30 Fr	30 Mo	30 We
31 Fr	31 Mo		31 Sa		31 Th

1994

January	February	March	April	May	June
1 Sa	1 Tu	1 Tu	1 Fr	1 Su	1 We
2 Su	2 We	2 We	2 Sa	2 Mo	2 Th
3 Mo	3 Th	3 Th	3 Su	3 Tu	3 Fr
4 Tu	4 Fr	4 Fr	4 Mo	4 We	4 Sa
5 We	5 Sa "Lazarus"	5 Sa	5 Tu	5 Th	5 Su
6 Th	6 Su	6 Su	6 We	6 Fr	6 Mo
7 Fr	7 Mo	7 Mo Scully's Anniversary	7 Th	7 Sa "The Erlenmeyer	7 Tu
8 Sa	8 Tu	8 Tu "Miracle Man" opens	8 Fr	8 Su Flask" opens	8 We
9 Su	9 We	9 Su -4 days	9 Sa	9 Sa	9 Th
10 Mo	10 Th	10 Th field work	10 Su	10 Tu The Erlenmeyer	10 Fr
11 Tu	11 Fr	11 Fr "Miracle Man" closes	11 Mo	11 We Flask "closes	11 Sa
12 We	12 Sa	12 Sa	12 Tu -Last	12 Th	12 Su
13 Th	13 Su	13 Su	13 We Case	13 Fr	13 Mo
14 Fr	14 Mo	14 Mo "Shapes"	14 Th Notes	14 Sa	14 Tu
15 Sa	15 Tu	15 Tu	15 Fr entered	15 Su	15 We
16 Su	16 We "Young At	16 We	16 Sa on April	16 Mo	16 Th
17 Mo	17 Th Heart"	17 Th	17 Su 19th/94	17 Tu	17 Fr
18 Tu	18 Fr	18 Fr	18 Mo	18 We	18 Sa
19 We	19 Sa	19 Sa "Darkness	19 Tu	19 Th	19 Su
20 Th	20 Su	20 Su Falls"	20 We	20 Fr	20 Mo
21 Fr	21 Mo	21 Mo Injury/ Quarantine	21 Th	21 Sa	21 Tu
22 Sa "Gender Bender"	22 Tu	22 Tu Time	22 Fr	22 Su	22 We
23 Su	23 We	23 We	23 Sa	23 Mo	23 Th
24 Mo	24 Th	24 Th "Tooms"	24 Su "Roland"	24 Tu	24 Fr
25 Tu	25 Fr	25 Fr	25 Mo -3 days	25 We	25 Sa
26 We	26 Sa "E.B.E"	26 Sa	26 Tu field work	26 Th	26 Su
27 Th	27 Su	27 Su "Born	27 We	27 Fr	27 Mo
28 Fr	28 Mo	28 Mo Again"	28 Th	28 Sa	28 Tu
29 Sa		29 Tu opens	29 Fr	29 Su	29 We
30 Su		30 We	30 Sa	30 Mo	30 Th
31 Mo		31 Th		31 Tu	

NO OFFICIAL INVESTIGATIONS

NO OFFICIAL INVESTIGATIONS

NO OFFICIAL INVESTIGATIONS

1994

January	February	March	April	May	June
1 Fr	1 Mo	1 Th	1 Sa X-Files on	1 Tu	1 Th
2 Sa	2 Tu	2 Fr	2 Su Special Agent	2 We	2 Fr 3:00-day???
3 Su	3 We "Little Green Men"	3 Sa	3 Mo Dana Scully	3 Th	3 Sa Quarantine00!
4 Mo	4 Th	4 Su	4 Tu opened by	4 Fr "One Breath" closes	4 Su
5 Tu	5 Fr	5 Mo	5 We Special Agent	5 Sa	5 Mo
6 We	6 Sa	6 Tu "Sleepless"	6 Th Mulder-	6 Su Agent Scully	6 Tu
7 Th	7 Su	7 We	7 Fr	7 Mo returns to active duty	7 We
8 Fr	8 Mo	8 Th	8 Sa	8 Tu	8 Th
9 Sa	9 Tu	9 Fr	9 Su	9 We	9 Fr
10 Su	10 We	10 Sa	10 Mo	10 Th	10 Sa
11 Mo	11 Th	11 Su	11 Tu	11 Fr	11 Su
12 Tu	12 Fr	12 Mo "Duane Barry"	12 We "3"	12 Sa "Firewalker"	12 Mo
13 We	13 Sa "The Host"	13 Tu	13 Th	13 Su "Firewalker"	13 Tu
14 Th	14 Su	14 We	14 Fr Case filed	14 Mo "Irresistible"	14 We
15 Fr	15 Mo	15 Th	15 Sa by F. Mulder/ LAPD	15 Tu	15 Th "Die Hand"
16 Sa	16 Tu	16 Fr	16 Su	16 We N.B.	16 Fr "Die verletzt"
17 Su	17 We	17 Sa "Ascension"	17 Mo	17 Th "Irresistible"	17 Sa
18 Mo	18 Th	18 Su	18 Tu	18 Fr case filed	18 Su
19 Tu	19 Fr	19 Mo	19 We	19 Sa during	19 Mo
20 We	20 Sa	20 Tu	20 Th	20 Su quarantine	20 Tu
21 Th	21 Su	21 We N.B. Scully listed as missing whereabouts unknown	21 Fr	21 Mo resulting	21 We "Fresh Bones"
22 Fr	22 Mo "Blood"	22 Th	22 Sa	22 Tu from	22 Th
23 Sa	23 Tu	23 Fr	23 Su	23 We "Firewalker"-	23 Fr
24 Su	24 We	24 Sa	24 Mo	24 Th as were	24 Sa
25 Mo	25 Th	25 Su	25 Tu	25 Fr "Red Museum",	25 Su
26 Tu	26 Fr	26 Mo	26 We	26 Sa "Excelsis Dei,	26 Mo
27 We	27 Sa	27 Tu	27 Th	27 Su & "Aubrey!"	27 Tu
28 Th	28 Su	28 We	28 Fr	28 Mo	28 We
29 Fr	29 Mo	29 Th	29 Sa "One Breath" opens	29 Tu	29 Th
30 Sa	30 Tu	30 Fr	30 Su	30 We	30 Fr
31 Su	31 We		31 Mo		31 Sa

NO OFFICIAL INVESTIGATIONS

1995

January	February	March	April	May	June
1 Su	1 We *"Colony"*	1 We	1 Sa	1 Mo	1 Th
2 Mo	2 Th *and*	2 Th	2 Su	2 Tu	2 Fr
3 Tu	3 Fr *"End Game"*	3 Fr	3 Mo *"Our Town"*	3 We	3 Sa
4 We	4 Sa *end*	4 Sa	4 Tu	4 Th	4 Su
5 Th	5 Su *Cases*	5 Su	5 We	5 Fr	5 Mo
6 Fr	6 Mo *"Fearful*	6 Mo	6 Th	6 Sa	6 Tu
7 Sa	7 Tu *Symmetry;"*	7 Tu	7 Fr	7 Su	7 We
8 Su	8 We *"Dod Kalm;"*	8 We	8 Sa	8 Mo	8 Th
9 Mo	9 Th *"Humbug;"*	9 Th	9 Su	9 Tu	9 Fr
10 Tu	10 Fr *"The Calusari"*	10 Fr	10 Mo *"Anasazi"*	10 We	10 Sa
11 We	11 Sa *"F. Emasculata"*	11 Sa	11 Tu *"The*	11 Th	11 Su
12 Th	12 Su *are all*	12 Su	12 We *Blessing*	12 Fr	12 Mo
13 Fr	13 Mo *investigated.*	13 Mo	13 Sa *Way"*	13 Sa	13 Tu
14 Sa	14 Tu *N.B. Total*	14 Tu	14 Fr *"Paper Clip"*	14 Su	14 We
15 Su	15 We *Case Days*	15 We	15 Sa	15 Mo	15 Th
16 Mo ↑ *"Colony"*	16 Th *Required is*	16 Th	16 Su	16 Tu	16 Fr
17 Tu *and*	17 Fr *greater than*	17 Fr ↑ *"Soft*	17 Mo	17 We	17 Sa
18 We *"End Game"*	18 Sa *the Actual*	18 Sa *Light"*	18 Tu	18 Th	18 Su
19 Th *open*	19 Su *Total Available Calendar*	19 Su *Victims*	19 We	19 Fr	19 Mo
20 Fr	20 Mo *Days!*	20 Mo *Die*	20 Th	20 Sa	20 Tu
21 Sa	21 Tu	21 Tu	21 Fr	21 Su	21 We
22 Su	22 We	22 We	22 Sa	22 Mo	22 Th
23 Mo	23 Th	23 Th	23 Su	23 Tu	23 Fr
24 Tu	24 Fr	24 Fr	24 Mo	24 We	24 Sa
25 We	25 Sa	25 Sa	25 Tu	25 Th	25 Su
26 Th	26 Su	26 Su	26 We	26 Fr	26 Mo
27 Fr	27 Mo	27 Mo	27 Th	27 Sa	27 Tu
28 Sa	28 Tu	28 Tu	28 Fr	28 Su	28 We
29 Su		29 We	29 Sa	29 Mo	29 Th
30 Mo		30 Th	30 Su	30 Tu	30 Fr
31 Tu		31 Fr ↓		31 We	

1995

JULY	AUGUST	SEPTEMBER	OCTOBER	NOVEMBER	DECEMBER
1 Sa	1 Tu	1 Fr	1 Su	1 We	1 Fr
2 Su	2 We	2 Sa	2 Mo	2 Th	2 Sa
3 Mo	3 Th	3 Su	3 Tu "The Walk" –2 days of field	3 Fr	3 Su
4 Tu	4 Fr	4 Mo	4 We investigation	4 Sa	4 Mo
5 We	5 Sa	5 Tu	5 Th	5 Su	5 Tu
6 Th	6 Su	6 We "2 SHY" closes	6 Fr	6 Mo	6 We
7 Fr	7 Mo	7 Th ↓	7 Sa	7 Tu	7 Th
8 Sa	8 Tu	8 Fr	8 Su	8 We	8 Fr
9 Su	9 We	9 Sa	9 Mo	9 Th	9 Sa
10 Mo	10 Th	10 Su	10 Tu "Oubliette"	10 Fr	10 Su
11 Tu	11 Fr	11 Mo "D.P.O" opens	11 We –4 days	11 Sa	11 Mo
12 We	12 Sa	12 Tu	12 Th of field	12 Su	12 Tu
13 Th	13 Su	13 We "D.P.O" closes	13 Fr assignment	13 Mo	13 We
14 Fr	14 Mo	14 Th	14 Sa	14 Tu	14 Th
15 Sa	15 Tu	15 Fr	15 Su	15 We	15 Fr
16 Su	16 We	16 Sa "Clyde Buckman's Final Repose" opens	16 Mo	16 Th	16 Sa
17 Mo	17 Th	17 Su	17 Tu "Nisei" &	17 Fr	17 Su
18 Tu	18 Fr	18 Mo	18 We "731" open	18 Sa	18 Mo
19 We	19 Sa	19 Tu	19 Th –4 days of	19 Su	19 Tu
20 Th	20 Su	20 We	20 Fr field work	20 Mo	20 We
21 Fr	21 Mo	21 Th	21 Sa with further	21 Tu "Revelations" opens	21 Th
22 Sa	22 Tu	22 Fr "Clyde Buckman's Final Repose" closes * N.B. Check that lottery ticket again!	22 Su week of	22 We	22 Fr
23 Su	23 We	23 Sa	23 Mo in-office	23 Th	23 Sa
24 Mo	24 Th	24 Su	24 Tu duty as well	24 Fr	24 Su
25 Tu	25 Fr	25 Mo	25 We as investigation	25 Sa	25 Mo
26 We	26 Sa	26 Tu	26 Th of various	26 Su	26 Tu
27 Th	27 Su	27 We "The List"	27 Fr documents.	27 Mo "Revelations" closes	27 We
28 Fr	28 Mo	28 Th	28 Sa	28 Tu	28 Th
29 Sa	29 Tu "2 SHY" opens ↑	29 Fr –3 days	29 Su	29 We	29 Fr
30 Su	30 We	30 Sa of on-site investigation	30 Mo	30 Th	30 Sa
31 Mo	31 Th		31 Tu		31 Su

1996

January	February	March	April	May	June
1 Mo "War of the	1 Th	1 Fr	1 Mo	1 We	1 Sa
2 Tu Coprophages" of	2 Fr	2 Sa	2 Tu	2 Th	2 Su
3 We	3 Sa "Pusher"	3 Su	3 We	3 Fr	3 Mo
4 Th -3 days of	4 Su -3 days of	4 Mo	4 Th	4 Sa	4 Tu
5 Fr field work	5 Mo hands-on investigation	5 Tu	5 Fr	5 Su	5 We
6 Sa	6 Tu	6 We	6 Sa	6 Mo	6 Th
7 Su	7 We	7 Th "Avatar" opens	7 Su	7 Tu	7 Fr
8 Mo	8 Th	8 Fr	8 Mo	8 We	8 Sa
9 Tu	9 Fr	9 Sa	9 Tu	9 Th	9 Su
10 We "Syzygy" opens	10 Sa "Teso dos	10 Su "Avatar"	10 We	10 Fr "Wet Wired" closes	10 Mo
11 Th	11 Su Bichos"	11 Mo closes	11 Th	11 Sa	11 Tu
12 Fr "Syzygy"	12 Mo -3 days of	12 Tu	12 Fr	12 Su	12 We
13 Sa closes	13 Tu field work	13 We	13 Sa	13 Mo "Talitha	13 Th
14 Su	14 We	14 Th "Quagmire"	14 Su	14 Tu Cumi"	14 Fr
15 Mo "Grotesque"	15 Th	15 Fr -2 days of	15 Mo	15 We -4 days	15 Sa
16 Tu -3 days of	16 Fr	16 Sa investigation	16 Tu	16 Th investigation	16 Su
17 We hands-on investigation	17 Sa "Hell Money"	17 Su	17 We	17 Fr	17 Mo
18 Th -3 weeks to	18 Su -3 days of	18 Mo	18 Th	18 Sa	18 Tu
19 Fr the incarceration	19 Mo field work	19 Tu	19 Fr W.W. murder #1	19 Su	19 We
20 Sa of Patterson	20 Tu	20 We	20 Sa	20 Mo	20 Th
21 Su	21 We	21 Th	21 Su W.W. murder #2	21 Tu	21 Fr
22 Mo	22 Th	22 Fr	22 Mo	22 We	22 Sa
23 Tu	23 Fr	23 Sa	23 Tu W.W. murder #3	23 Th	23 Su
24 We	24 Sa "Jose Chung's	24 Su	24 We	24 Fr	24 Mo
25 Th	25 Su 'From	25 Mo	25 Th	25 Sa	25 Tu
26 Fr "Piper Maru"	26 Mo Outer Space"	26 Tu	26 Fr	26 Su	26 We
27 Sa and "Apocrypha"	27 Tu -7 days	27 We	27 Sa "Wet Wired"	27 Mo	27 Th
28 Su open	28 We on-site field	28 Th	28 Su opens	28 Tu	28 Fr
29 Mo -10 days of hands-on	29 Th investigations	29 Fr	29 Mo	29 We	29 Sa
30 Tu investigation		30 Sa	30 Tu	30 Th	30 Su
31 We		31 Su		31 Fr	

1996

July	August	September	October	November	December
1 Mo	1 Th	1 Su	1 Tu	1 Fr	1 Su
2 Tu	2 Fr	2 Mo	2 We	2 Sa	2 Mo
3 We	3 Sa	3 Tu	3 Th	3 Su	3 Tu
4 Th	4 Su	4 We	4 Fr	4 Mo	4 We
5 Fr	5 Mo	5 Th	5 Sa	5 Tu	5 Th
6 Sa	6 Tu	6 Fr	6 Su	6 We	6 Fr
7 Su	7 We	7 Sa	7 Mo	7 Th	7 Sa
8 Mo	8 Th	8 Su	8 Tu	8 Fr	8 Su
9 Tu	9 Fr	9 Mo	9 We	9 Sa	9 Mo
10 We	10 Sa	10 Tu	10 Th	10 Su	10 Tu
11 Th	11 Su	11 We	11 Fr	11 Mo	11 We
12 Fr	12 Mo	12 Th	12 Sa	12 Tu	12 Th
13 Sa	13 Tu	13 Fr	13 Su	13 We	13 Fr
14 Su	14 We	14 Sa	14 Mo	14 Th	14 Sa
15 Mo	15 Th	15 Su	15 Tu	15 Fr	15 Su
16 Tu	16 Fr	16 Mo	16 We	16 Sa	16 Mo
17 We	17 Sa	17 Tu	17 Th	17 Su	17 Tu
18 Th	18 Su	18 We	18 Fr	18 Mo	18 We
19 Fr	19 Mo	19 Th	19 Sa	19 Tu	19 Th
20 Sa	20 Tu	20 Fr	20 Su	20 We	20 Fr
21 Su	21 We	21 Sa	21 Mo	21 Th	21 Sa
22 Mo	22 Th	22 Su	22 Tu	22 Fr	22 Su
23 Tu	23 Fr	23 Mo	23 We	23 Sa	23 Mo
24 We	24 Sa	24 Tu	24 Th	24 Su	24 Tu
25 Th	25 Su	25 We	25 Fr	25 Mo	25 We
26 Fr	26 Mo	26 Th	26 Sa	26 Tu	26 Th
27 Sa	27 Tu	27 Fr	27 Su	27 We	27 Fr
28 Su	28 We	28 Sa	28 Mo	28 Th	28 Sa
29 Mo	29 Th	29 Su	29 Tu	29 Fr	29 Su
30 Tu	30 Fr	30 Mo	30 We	30 Sa	30 Mo
31 We	31 Sa		31 Th		31 Tu

☒ PHONE/ADDRESSES ☒

Duane Barry's Travel Agency
555-8295

N.B.: *Check their rates, too . . .*

Danny Bernstein
1-202-555-4524 (FAX ONLY)
c/o FBI Headquarters
Cryptography Section
Washington, DC

N.B.: *Hang up if supervisor answers!*

Dr. Terrence Berubi
1-301-555-1517

Dateline
1-900-555-0198

N.B.: *Check that first-minute rate. Pass along to guys in Vice.*

Elizabeth
555-6936
925 August Street

N.B.: *Girlfriend of escaped prisoner. Hold under surveillance pending possible contact.*

FBI Hotline Number

Lula Phillips Case
1-800-555-4040
See FBIHQ, Washington.

N.B.: *Render number inactive in 90 days.*

FBI Hotline Number

Virgil Incanto Case
1-800-555-0312
See FBIHQ, Washington.

N.B.: *Render number inactive in 90 days.*

Paula Gray

1-501-555-7265
Dudley, Arkansas

N.B.: *Check D.O.B. on employment forms.*

Home Value Network

1-800-555-8300

N.B.: *Gotta get that "Little Traveler"!*

Robert Modell, AKA Pusher

1-703-555-0146
1-703-555-0118
1-703-555-0177
1-703-555-0197 (pay phone)

John L. Mostow

1214 Harold Street
Washington, DC
also 1222 South Dakota Street
Washington, DC

Fox William Mulder

1-202-555-0199

Samantha T. Mulder

LAST KNOWN ADDRESS
2790 Vine Street
Chilmarc(k), MA
aka Samantha ANNE Mulder

William Mulder

62 Greer Street
West Tisbury
Martha's Vineyard

N.B.: *Past agent with State Department*

Greg Nemhauser, Special Agent

1-202-555-0143 (cell phone only)

Jeremiah Smith

3813 Bay Bridge Avenue
New York, NY 10001

Jeremiah Smith

#7, 1012 Beckwith
Miami, FL 33101

THE Consortium

1-212-555-1012
46th Street
New York, NY

N.B.: *Line is likely disconnected.*

Det. Angela White

1-603-555-0114
Comity, Caryl County

N.B.: *VERY helpful!*

Women's Health Services Clinic

1235 91st Street
Rockville, MD

Yappi, the Stupendous

1-900-555-YAPP

N.B.: *A mere $4.95 for the first minute!*

Dr. Shiro Zama, AKA Dr. Ishi Maru

1-304-555-0103
c/o Hansen Center for Disease Control
R.R. 1
Perkey, WV 26301

Zeus Storage

1-301-555-2804
1616 Pandora
Maryland

N.B.: *Check on rates for long-term clients!*